STATE AND REVOLUTION

BY
V. I. LENIN

INTERNATIONAL PUBLISHERS
NEW YORK

CONTENTS

PREFACE TO FIRST EDITION [1]

THE question of the state is acquiring at present a particular importance, both as theory, and from the point of view of practical politics. The imperialist war has greatly accelerated and intensified the transformation of monopoly capitalism into state-monopoly capitalism. The monstrous oppression of the labouring masses by the state—which connects itself more and more intimately with the all-powerful capitalist combines—is becoming ever more monstrous. The foremost countries are being converted—we speak here of their "rear"—into military convict labour prisons for the workers.

The unheard-of horrors and miseries of the protracted war are making the position of the masses unbearable and increasing their indignation. An international proletarian revolution is clearly rising. The question of its relation to the state is acquiring a practical importance.

The elements of opportunism accumulated during the decades of comparatively peaceful development have created a predominance of social-chauvinism in the official Socialist parties of the whole world (Plekhanov, Potresov, Breshkovskaya, Rubanovich, and, in a slightly concealed form, Messrs. Tsereteli, Chernov and Co., in Russia; Scheidemann, Legien, David and others in Germany; Renaudel, Guesde, Vandervelde in France and Belgium; Hyndman and the Fabians in England, etc., etc.). Socialism in words, chauvinism in deeds is characterised by a base, servile adaptation of the "leaders of Socialism" to the interests not only of "their" national bourgeoisie, but also of "their" state—for a whole series of smaller, weaker nationalities have long since been exploited and enslaved by most of the so-called great powers. The imperialist war is just a war for division and re-division of this kind of booty. The struggle for the emancipation of the labouring masses from the influence of the bourgeoisie in general, and the imperialist bourgeoisie in particular, is impossible without a struggle against the opportunist superstitions concerning the "state."

We first of all survey the teachings of Marx and Engels on the state, dwelling with particular fullness on those aspects of their teachings which have been forgotten or opportunistically distorted. We then analyse specially the chief representative of these distorters, Karl Kautsky, the best known leader of the Second International (1889-1914), who has suffered such a pitiful political bankruptcy during the present war. Finally, we sum up, in the main, the experiences of the Russian Revolution of 1905 and particularly that of 1917. The revolution is evidently completing at the present time (beginning of August, 1917) the first stage of its development; but, generally speaking, this revolution can be understood in its totality only as a link in the chain of Socialist proletarian revolutions called forth by the imperialist war. The question of the relation of a proletarian Socialist revolution to the state acquires, therefore, not only a practical political importance, but the importance of an urgent problem of the day, the problem of elucidating to the masses what they will have to do for their liberation from the yoke of capitalism in the very near future.

THE AUTHOR.

August, 1917.

PREFACE TO SECOND EDITION

THE present, second, edition is published almost without change. Paragraph three has been added to Chapter II.

THE AUTHOR.

Moscow, December 30, 1918.

STATE AND REVOLUTION

CHAPTER I

CLASS SOCIETY AND THE STATE

1. The State as the Product of the Irreconcilability of Class Antagonisms

WHAT is now happening to Marx's doctrine has, in the course of history, often happened to the doctrines of other revolutionary thinkers and leaders of oppressed classes struggling for emancipation. During the lifetime of great revolutionaries, the oppressing classes have visited relentless persecution on them and received their teaching with the most savage hostility, the most furious hatred, the most ruthless campaign of lies and slanders. After their death, attempts are made to turn them into harmless icons, canonise them, and surround their *names* with a certain halo for the "consolation" of the oppressed classes and with the object of duping them, while at the same time emasculating and vulgarising the *real essence* of their revolutionary theories and blunting their revolutionary edge. At the present time, the bourgeoisie and the opportunists within the labour movement are co-operating in this work of adulterating Marxism. They omit, obliterate, and distort the revolutionary side of its teaching, its revolutionary soul. They push to the foreground and extol what is, or seems, acceptable to the bourgeoisie. All the social-chauvinists are now "Marxists"—joking aside! And more and more do German bourgeois professors, erstwhile specialists in the demolition of Marx, speak now of the "national-German" Marx, who, they aver, has educated the labour unions which are so splendidly organised for conducting the present predatory war!

In such circumstances, the distortion of Marxism being so widespread, it is our first task to *resuscitate* the real teachings of Marx on the state. For this purpose it will be necessary to quote at length from the works of Marx and Engels themselves. Of course, long quotations will make the text cumbersome and in no way help to make it popular reading, but we cannot possibly avoid them. All, or at any rate, all the most essential passages in the works of Marx and Engels on the subject of the state must necessarily be given as fully as possible, in order that the reader may form an independent opinion of all the views of the founders of scientific Socialism and of the development of those views, and in order that their distortions by the present predominant "Kautskyism" may be proved in black and white and rendered plain to all.

Let us begin with the most popular of Engels' works, *Der Ursprung der Familie, des Privateigentums und des Staats,** the sixth edition of which was published in Stuttgart as far back as 1894. We must translate the quotations from the German originals, as the Russian translations, although very numerous, are for the most part either incomplete or very unsatisfactory.

Summarising his historical analysis Engels says:

> The state is therefore by no means a power imposed on society from the outside; just as little is it "the reality of the moral idea," "the image and reality of reason," as Hegel asserted. Rather, it is a product of society at a certain stage of development; it is the admission that this society has become entangled in an insoluble contradiction with itself, that it is cleft into irreconcilable antagonisms which it is powerless to dispel. But in order that these antagonisms, classes with conflicting economic interests, may not consume themselves and society in sterile struggle, a power apparently standing above society becomes necessary, whose purpose is to moderate the conflict and keep it within the bounds of "order"; and this power arising out of society, but placing itself above it, and increasingly separating itself from it, is the state.**

Here we have, expressed in all its clearness, the basic idea of Marxism on the question of the historical rôle and meaning of the state. The state is the product and the manifestation of the *irreconcilability* of class antagonisms. The state arises when, where, and to the extent that the class antagonisms *cannot* be objectively reconciled. And, conversely, the existence of the state proves that the class antagonisms *are* irreconcilable.

It is precisely on this most important and fundamental point that distortions of Marxism arise along two main lines.

On the one hand, the bourgeois, and particularly the petty-bourgeois, ideologists, compelled under the pressure of indisputable historical facts to admit that the state only exists where there are class antagonisms and the class struggle, "correct" Marx in such a

---

* Friedrich Engels, *The Origin of the Family, Private Property, and the State,* London and New York, 1933.—*Ed.*
** *Ibid.*—*Ed.*

way as to make it appear that the state is an organ for *reconciling* the classes. According to Marx, the state could neither arise nor maintain itself if a reconciliation of classes were possible. But with the petty-bourgeois and philistine professors and publicists, the state—and this frequently on the strength of benevolent references to Marx!—becomes a conciliator of the classes. According to Marx, the state is an organ of class *domination,* an organ of *oppression* of one class by another; its aim is the creation of "order" which legalises and perpetuates this oppression by moderating the collisions between the classes. But in the opinion of the petty-bourgeois politicians, order means reconciliation of the classes, and not oppression of one class by another; to moderate collisions does not mean, they say, to deprive the oppressed classes of certain definite means and methods of struggle for overthrowing the oppressors, but to practice reconciliation.

For instance, when, in the Revolution of 1917, the question of the real meaning and rôle of the state arose in all its vastness as a practical question demanding immediate action on a wide mass scale, all the Socialist-Revolutionaries and Mensheviks suddenly and completely sank to the petty-bourgeois theory of "reconciliation" of the classes by the "state." Innumerable resolutions and articles by politicians of both these parties are saturated through and through with this purely petty-bourgeois and philistine theory of "reconciliation." That the state is an organ of domination of a definite class which *cannot* be reconciled with its antipode (the class opposed to it)—this petty-bourgeois democracy is never able to understand. Its attitude towards the state is one of the most telling proofs that our Socialist-Revolutionaries and Mensheviks are not Socialists at all (which we Bolsheviks have always maintained), but petty-bourgeois democrats with a near-Socialist phraseology.

On the other hand, the "Kautskyist" distortion of Marx is far more subtle. "Theoretically," there is no denying that the state is the organ of class domination, or that class antagonisms are irreconcilable. But what is forgotten or glossed over is this: if the state is the product of the irreconcilable character of class antagonisms, if it is a force standing *above* society and "increasingly separating itself from it," then it is clear that the liberation of the oppressed class is impossible not only without a violent revolution, *but also without the destruction* of the apparatus of state power, which was created by the ruling class and in which this "separation" is embodied. As we shall see later, Marx drew this theoretically self-evident conclusion from a concrete historical analysis of the problems of revolution. And it is exactly this conclusion which Kautsky—as we shall show fully in our subsequent remarks—has "forgotten" and distorted.

2. Special Bodies of Armed Men, Prisons, Etc.

Engels continues:

> In contrast with the ancient organisation of the *gens*, the first distinguishing characteristic of the state is the grouping of the subjects of the state *on a territorial basis*. . . .

Such a grouping seems "natural" to us, but it came after a prolonged and costly struggle against the old form of tribal or gentilic society.

> . . . The second is the establishment of a *public force*, which is no longer absolutely identical with the population organising itself as an armed power. This special public force is necessary, because a self-acting armed organisation of the population has become impossible since the cleavage of society into classes. . . . This public force exists in every state; it consists not merely of armed men, but of material appendages, prisons and repressive institutions of all kinds, of which gentilic society knew nothing. . . .*

Engels develops the conception of that "power" which is termed the state—a power arising from society, but placing itself above it and becoming more and more separated from it. What does this power mainly consist of? It consists of special bodies of armed men who have at their disposal prisons, etc.

We are justified in speaking of special bodies of armed men, because the public power peculiar to every state is not "absolutely identical" with the armed population, with its "self-acting armed organisation."

Like all the great revolutionary thinkers, Engels tries to draw the attention of the class-conscious workers to that very fact which to prevailing philistinism appears least of all worthy of attention, most common and sanctified by solid, indeed, one might say, petrified prejudices. A standing army and police are the chief instruments of state power. But can this be otherwise?

From the point of view of the vast majority of Europeans at the end of the nineteenth century whom Engels was addressing, and who had neither lived through nor closely observed a single great

* *Ibid.—Ed.*

revolution, this cannot be otherwise. They cannot understand at all what this "self-acting armed organisation of the population" means. To the question, whence arose the need for special bodies of armed men, standing above society and becoming separated from it (police and standing army), the Western European and Russian philistines are inclined to answer with a few phrases borrowed from Spencer or Mikhailovsky, by reference to the complexity of social life, the differentiation of functions, and so forth.

Such a reference seems "scientific" and effectively dulls the senses of the average man, obscuring the most important and basic fact, namely, the break-up of society into irreconcilably antagonistic classes.

Without such a break-up, the "self-acting armed organisation of the population" might have differed from the primitive organisation of a herd of monkeys grasping sticks, or of primitive men, or men united in a tribal form of society, by its complexity, its high technique, and so forth, but would still have been possible.

It is impossible now, because society, in the period of civilisation, is broken up into antagonistic and, indeed, irreconcilably antagonistic classes, which, if armed in a "self-acting" manner, would come into armed struggle with each other. A state is formed, a special power is created in the form of special bodies of armed men, and every revolution, by shattering the state apparatus, demonstrates to us how the ruling class aims at the restoration of the special bodies of armed men at *its* service, and how the oppressed class tries to create a new organisation of this kind, capable of serving not the exploiters, but the exploited.

In the above observation, Engels raises theoretically the very same question which every great revolution raises practically, palpably, and on a mass scale of action, namely, the question of the relation between special bodies of armed men and the "self-acting armed organisation of the population." We shall see how this is concretely illustrated by the experience of the European and Russian revolutions.

But let us return to Engels' discourse.

He points out that sometimes, for instance, here and there in North America, this public power is weak (he has in mind an exception that is rare in capitalist society, and he speaks about parts of North America in its pre-imperialist days, where the free colonist predominated), but that in general it tends to become stronger:

It [the public power] grows stronger, however, in proportion as the class antagonisms within the state grow sharper, and with the growth in size and population of the adjacent states. We have only to look at our present-day Europe, where class struggle and rivalry in conquest have screwed up the public power to such a pitch that it threatens to devour the whole of society and even the state itself.*

This was written as early as the beginning of the 'nineties of last century, Engels' last preface being dated June 16, 1891. The turn towards imperialism, understood to mean complete domination of the trusts, full sway of the large banks, and a colonial policy on a grand scale, and so forth, was only just beginning in France, and was even weaker in North America and in Germany. Since then the "rivalry in conquest" has made gigantic progress—especially as, by the beginning of the second decade of the twentieth century, the whole world had been finally divided up between these "rivals in conquest," *i.e.*, between the great predatory powers. Military and naval armaments since then have grown to monstrous proportions, and the predatory war of 1914-1917 for the domination of the world by England or Germany, for the division of the spoils, has brought the "swallowing up" of all the forces of society by the rapacious state power nearer to a complete catastrophe.

As early as 1891 Engels was able to point to "rivalry in conquest" as one of the most important features of the foreign policy of the great powers, but in 1914-1917, when this rivalry, many times intensified, has given birth to an imperialist war, the rascally social-chauvinists cover up their defence of the predatory policy of "their" capitalist classes by phrases about the "defence of the fatherland," or the "defence of the republic and the revolution," etc.!

3. THE STATE AS AN INSTRUMENT FOR THE EXPLOITATION OF THE OPPRESSED CLASS

For the maintenance of a special public force standing above society, taxes and state loans are needed.

Having at their disposal the public force and the right to exact taxes, the officials now stand as organs of society *above* society. The free, voluntary respect which was accorded to the organs of the gentilic form of government does not satisfy them, even if they could have it. . . .

Special laws are enacted regarding the sanctity and the inviolability of the officials. "The shabbiest police servant . . . has

* *Ibid.—Ed.*

more authority" than the representative of the clan, but even the head of the military power of a civilised state "may well envy the least among the chiefs of the clan the unconstrained and uncontested respect which is paid to him." *

Here the question regarding the privileged position of the officials as organs of state power is clearly stated. The main point is indicated as follows: what is it that places them *above* society? We shall see how this theoretical problem was solved in practice by the Paris Commune in 1871 and how it was slurred over in a reactionary manner by Kautsky in 1912.

As the state arose out of the need to hold class antagonisms in check; but as it, at the same time, arose in the midst of the conflict of these classes, it is, as a rule, the state of the most powerful, economically dominant class, which by virtue thereof becomes also the dominant class politically, and thus acquires new means of holding down and exploiting the oppressed class. . . .

Not only the ancient and feudal states were organs of exploitation of the slaves and serfs, but

the modern representative state is the instrument of the exploitation of wage-labour by capital. By way of exception, however, there are periods when the warring classes so nearly attain equilibrium that the state power, ostensibly appearing as a mediator, assumes for the moment a certain independence in relation to both. . . .**

Such were, for instance, the absolute monarchies of the seventeenth and eighteenth centuries, the Bonapartism of the First and Second Empires in France, and the Bismarck régime in Germany.

Such, we may add, is now the Kerensky government in republican Russia after its shift to persecuting the revolutionary proletariat, at a moment when the Soviets, thanks to the leadership of the petty-bourgeois democrats, have *already* become impotent, while the bourgeoisie is *not yet* strong enough to disperse them outright.

In a democratic republic, Engels continues, "wealth wields its power indirectly, but all the more effectively," first, by means of "direct corruption of the officials" (America); second, by means of "the alliance of the government with the stock exchange" (France and America).

At the present time, imperialism and the domination of the banks have "developed" to an unusually fine art both these methods of defending and asserting the omnipotence of wealth in democratic republics of all descriptions. If, for instance, in the very first months

* *Ibid.—Ed.*   ** *Ibid.—Ed.*

of the Russian democratic republic, one might say during the honey-moon of the union of the "Socialists"—Socialist-Revolutionaries and Mensheviks—with the bourgeoisie, Mr. Palchinsky obstructed every measure in the coalition cabinet, restraining the capitalists and their war profiteering, their plundering of the public treasury by means of army contracts; and if, after his resignation, Mr. Palchinsky (replaced, of course, by an exactly similar Palchinsky) was "rewarded" by the capitalists with a "soft" job carrying a salary of 120,000 rubles per annum, what was this? Direct or indirect bribery? A league of the government with the capitalist syndicates, or "only" friendly relations? What is the rôle played by the Chernovs, Tseretelis, Avksentyevs and Skobelevs? Are they the "direct" or only the indirect allies of the millionaire treasury looters?

The omnipotence of "wealth" is thus more *secure* in a democratic republic, since it does not depend on the poor political shell of capitalism. A democratic republic is the best possible political shell for capitalism, and therefore, once capital has gained control (through the Palchinskys, Chernovs, Tseretelis and Co.) of this very best shell, it establishes its power so securely, so firmly that *no* change, either of persons, or institutions, or parties in the bourgeois republic can shake it.

We must also note that Engels quite definitely regards universal suffrage as a means of bourgeois domination. Universal suffrage, he says, obviously summing up the long experience of German Social-Democracy, is "an index of the maturity of the working class; it cannot, and never will, be anything else but that in the modern state."

The petty-bourgeois democrats, such as our Socialist-Revolution-aries and Mensheviks, and also their twin brothers, the social-chauvinists and opportunists of Western Europe, all expect "more" from universal suffrage. They themselves share, and instil into the minds of the people, the wrong idea that universal suffrage "in the *modern* state" is really capable of expressing the will of the majority of the toilers and of assuring its realisation.

We can here only note this wrong idea, only point out that this perfectly clear, exact and concrete statement by Engels is distorted at every step in the propaganda and agitation of the "official" (*i.e.*, opportunist) Socialist parties. A detailed analysis of all the false-ness of this idea, which Engels brushes aside, is given in our further account of the views of Marx and Engels on the "modern" state.

14

A general summary of his views is given by Engels
popular of his works in the following words:

The state, therefore, has not existed from all eternity. T
societies which managed without it, which had no conception
state power. At a certain stage of economic development, which was nec̶e̶s̶s̶
bound up with the cleavage of society into classes, the state became a necessity
owing to this cleavage. We are now rapidly approaching a stage in the development of production at which the existence of these classes has not only
ceased to be a necessity, but is becoming a positive hindrance to production.
They will disappear as inevitably as they arose at an earlier stage. Along with
them, the state will inevitably disappear. The society that organises production anew on the basis of a free and equal association of the producers will put
the whole state machine where it will then belong: in the museum of antiquities,
side by side with the spinning wheel and the bronze axe.*

It is not often that we find this passage quoted in the propaganda
and agitation literature of contemporary Social-Democracy. But
even when we do come across it, it is generally quoted in the same
manner as one bows before an icon, *i.e.*, it is done merely to show
official respect for Engels, without any attempt to gauge the breadth
and depth of revolutionary action presupposed by this relegating
of "the whole state machine . . . to the museum of antiquities." In
most cases we do not even find an understanding of what Engels
calls the state machine.

4. The "Withering Away" of the State and Violent Revolution

Engels' words regarding the "withering away" of the state enjoy
such popularity, they are so often quoted, and they show so clearly
the essence of the usual adulteration by means of which Marxism
is made to look like opportunism, that we must dwell on them in
detail. Let us quote the whole passage from which they are taken.

The proletariat seizes state power, and then transforms the means of production into state property. But in doing this, it puts an end to itself as the
proletariat, it puts an end to all class differences and class antagonisms, it puts
an end also to the state as the state. Former society, moving in class antagonisms, had need of the state, that is, an organisation of the exploiting class at
each period for the maintenance of its external conditions of production; therefore, in particular, for the forcible holding down of the exploited class in the
conditions of oppression (slavery, bondage or serfdom, wage-labour) determined
by the existing mode of production. The state was the official representative of
society as a whole, its embodiment in a visible corporate body; but it was this
only in so far as it was the state of that class which itself, in its epoch, repre-

* *Ibid.—Ed.*

15

.ed society as a whole: in ancient times, the state of the slave-owning ιtizens; in the Middle Ages, of the feudal nobility; in our epoch, of the bourgeoisie. When ultimately it becomes really representative of society as a whole, it makes itself superfluous. As soon as there is no longer any class of society to be held in subjection; as soon as, along with class domination and the struggle for individual existence based on the former anarchy of production, the collisions and excesses arising from these have also been abolished, there is nothing more to be repressed, and a special repressive force, a state, is no longer necessary. The first act in which the state really comes forward as the representative of society as a whole—the seizure of the means of production in the name of society—is at the same time its last independent act as a state. The interference of a state power in social relations becomes superfluous in one sphere after another, and then becomes dormant of itself. Government over persons is replaced by the administration of things and the direction of the processes of production. The state is not "abolished," *it withers away.* It is from this standpoint that we must appraise the phrase "people's free state"—both its justification at times for agitational purposes, and its ultimate scientific inadequacy—and also the demand of the so-called Anarchists that the state should be abolished overnight.*

Without fear of committing an error, it may be said that of this argument by Engels so singularly rich in ideas, only one point has become an integral part of Socialist thought among modern Socialist parties, namely, that, unlike the Anarchist doctrine of the "abolition" of the state, according to Marx the state "withers away." To emasculate Marxism in such a manner is to reduce it to opportunism, for such an "interpretation" only leaves the hazy conception of a slow, even, gradual change, free from leaps and storms, free from revolution. The current popular conception, if one may say so, of the "withering away" of the state undoubtedly means a slurring over, if not a negation, of revolution.

Yet, such an "interpretation" is the crudest distortion of Marxism, which is advantageous only to the bourgeoisie; in point of theory, it is based on a disregard for the most important circumstances and considerations pointed out in the very passage summarising Engels' ideas, which we have just quoted in full.

In the first place, Engels at the very outset of his argument says that, in assuming state power, the proletariat by that very act "puts an end to the state as the state." One is "not accustomed" to reflect on what this really means. Generally, it is either ignored altogether, or it is considered as a piece of "Hegelian weakness" on Engels' part. As a matter of fact, however, these words express succinctly the experience of one of the greatest proletarian revolutions—the Paris Commune of 1871, of which we shall speak in greater detail

* Friedrich Engels, *Anti-Dühring*, London and New York, 1933.—*Ed.*

in its proper place. As a matter of fact, Engels speaks here of the destruction of the bourgeois state by the proletarian revolution, while the words about its withering away refer to the remains of *proletarian* statehood *after* the Socialist revolution. The bourgeois state does not "wither away," according to Engels, but is "put an end to" by the proletariat in the course of the revolution. What withers away after the revolution is the proletarian state or semi-state.

Secondly, the state is a "special repressive force." This splendid and extremely profound definition of Engels' is given by him here with complete lucidity. It follows from this that the "special repressive force" of the bourgeoisie for the suppression of the proletariat, of the millions of workers by a handful of the rich, must be replaced by a "special repressive force" of the proletariat for the suppression of the bourgeoisie (the dictatorship of the proletariat). It is just this that constitutes the destruction of "the state as the state." It is just this that constitutes the "act" of "the seizure of the means of production in the name of society." And it is obvious that such a substitution of one (proletarian) "special repressive force" for another (bourgeois) "special repressive force" can in no way take place in the form of a "withering away."

Thirdly, as to the "withering away" or, more expressively and colourfully, as to the state "becoming dormant," Engels refers quite clearly and definitely to the period *after* "the seizure of the means of production [by the state] in the name of society," that is, *after* the Socialist revolution. We all know that the political form of the "state" at that time is complete democracy. But it never enters the head of any of the opportunists who shamelessly distort Marx that when Engels speaks here of the state "withering away," or "becoming dormant," he speaks of *democracy*. At first sight this seems very strange. But it is "unintelligible" only to one who has not reflected on the fact that democracy is *also* a state and that, consequently, democracy will *also* disappear when the state disappears. The bourgeois state can only be "put an end to" by a revolution. The state in general, *i.e.*, most complete democracy, can only "wither away."

Fourthly, having formulated his famous proposition that "the state withers away," Engels at once explains concretely that this proposition is directed equally against the opportunists and the Anarchists. In doing this, however, Engels puts in the first place that conclusion from his proposition about the "withering away" of the state which is directed against the opportunists.

One can wager that out of every 10,000 persons who have read or heard about the "withering away" of the state, 9,990 do not know at all, or do not remember, that Engels did not direct his conclusions from this proposition against the Anarchists *alone*. And out of the remaining ten, probably nine do not know the meaning of a "people's free state" nor the reason why an attack on this watchword contains an attack on the opportunists. This is how history is written! This is how a great revolutionary doctrine is imperceptibly adulterated and adapted to current philistinism! The conclusion drawn against the Anarchists has been repeated thousands of times, vulgarised, harangued about in the crudest fashion possible until it has acquired the strength of a prejudice, whereas the conclusion drawn against the opportunists has been hushed up and "forgotten"!

The "people's free state" was a demand in the programme of the German Social-Democrats and their current slogan in the 'seventies. There is no political substance in this slogan other than a pompous middle-class circumlocution of the idea of democracy. In so far as it referred in a lawful manner to a democratic republic, Engels was prepared to "justify" its use "at times" from a propaganda point of view. But this slogan was opportunist, for it not only expressed an exaggerated view of the attractiveness of bourgeois democracy, but also a lack of understanding of the Socialist criticism of every state in general. We are in favour of a democratic republic as the best form of the state for the proletariat under capitalism, but we have no right to forget that wage slavery is the lot of the people even in the most democratic bourgeois republic. Furthermore, every state is a "special repressive force" for the suppression of the oppressed class. Consequently, *no* state is either "free" or a "people's state." Marx and Engels explained this repeatedly to their party comrades in the 'seventies.

Fifthly, in the same work of Engels, from which every one remembers his argument on the "withering away" of the state, there is also a disquisition on the significance of a violent revolution. The historical analysis of its rôle becomes, with Engels, a veritable panegyric on violent revolution. This, of course, "no one remembers"; to talk or even to think of the importance of this idea is not considered good form by contemporary Socialist parties, and in the daily propaganda and agitation among the masses it plays no part whatever. Yet it is indissolubly bound up with the "withering away" of the state in one harmonious whole.

Here is Engels' argument:

> . . . That force, however, plays another rôle (other than that of a diabolical power) in history, a revolutionary rôle; that, in the words of Marx, it is the midwife of every old society which is pregnant with the new; that it is the instrument with whose aid social movement forces its way through and shatters the dead, fossilised political forms—of this there is not a word in Herr Dühring. It is only with sighs and groans that he admits the possibility that force will perhaps be necessary for the overthrow of the economic system of exploitation— unfortunately! because all use of force, forsooth, demoralises the person who uses it. And this in spite of the immense moral and spiritual impetus which has resulted from every victorious revolution! And this in Germany, where a violent collision—which indeed may be forced on the people—would at least have the advantage of wiping out the servility which has permeated the national consciousness as a result of the humiliation of the Thirty Years' War.[2] And this parson's mode of thought—lifeless, insipid and impotent—claims to impose itself on the most revolutionary party which history has known? *

How can this panegyric on violent revolution, which Engels insistently brought to the attention of the German Social-Democrats between 1878 and 1894, i.e., right to the time of his death, be combined with the theory of the "withering away" of the state to form one doctrine?

Usually the two views are combined by means of eclecticism, by an unprincipled, sophistic, arbitrary selection (to oblige the powers that be) of either one or the other argument, and in ninety-nine cases out of a hundred (if not more often), it is the idea of the "withering away" that is specially emphasised. Eclecticism is substituted for dialectics—this is the most usual, the most widespread phenomenon to be met with in the official Social-Democratic literature of our day in relation to Marxism. Such a substitution is, of course, nothing new; it may be observed even in the history of classic Greek philosophy. When Marxism is adulterated to become opportunism, the substitution of eclecticism for dialectics is the best method of deceiving the masses; it gives an illusory satisfaction; it seems to take into account all sides of the process, all the tendencies of development, all the contradictory factors and so forth, whereas in reality it offers no consistent and revolutionary view of the process of social development at all.

We have already said above and shall show more fully later that the teaching of Marx and Engels regarding the inevitability of a

* *Ibid.—Ed.*

violent revolution refers to the bourgeois state. It *cannot* be replaced by the proletarian state (the dictatorship of the proletariat) through "withering away," but, as a general rule, only through a violent revolution. The panegyric sung in its honour by Engels and fully corresponding to the repeated declarations of Marx (remember the concluding passages of the *Poverty of Philosophy* and the *Communist Manifesto*, with its proud and open declaration of the inevitability of a violent revolution; remember Marx's *Critique of the Gotha Programme* of 1875 in which, almost thirty years later, he mercilessly castigates the opportunist character of that programme [3])—this praise is by no means a mere "impulse," a mere declamation, or a polemical sally. The necessity of systematically fostering among the masses *this* and just this point of view about violent revolution lies at the root of the *whole* of Marx's and Engels' teaching. The neglect of such propaganda and agitation by both the present predominant social-chauvinist and the Kautskyist currents brings their betrayal of Marx's and Engels' teaching into prominent relief.

The replacement of the bourgeois by the proletarian state is impossible without a violent revolution. The abolition of the proletarian state, *i.e.*, of all states, is only possible through "withering away."

Marx and Engels gave a full and concrete exposition of these views in studying each revolutionary situation separately, in analysing the lessons of the experience of each individual revolution. We now pass to this, undoubtedly the most important part of their work.

CHAPTER II

THE EXPERIENCES OF 1848-1851

1. ON THE EVE OF REVOLUTION

THE first productions of mature Marxism—the *Poverty of Philosophy* and the *Communist Manifesto*—were created on the very eve of the Revolution of 1848. For this reason we have in them, side by side with a statement of the general principles of Marxism, a reflection, to a certain degree, of the concrete revolutionary situation of the time. Consequently, it will possibly be more to the point to examine what the authors of these works say about the state immediately before they draw conclusions from the experience of the years 1848-1851.

In the course of its development,—wrote Marx in the *Poverty of Philosophy*— the working class will replace the old bourgeois society by an association which excludes classes and their antagonism, and there will no longer be any real political power, for political power is precisely the official expression of the class antagonism within bourgeois society.*

It is instructive to compare with this general statement of the idea of the state disappearing after classes have disappeared, the statement contained in the *Communist Manifesto*, written by Marx and Engels a few months later—to be exact, in November, 1847:

In depicting the most general phases of the development of the proletariat, we traced the more or less veiled civil war, raging within existing society, up to the point where that war breaks out into open revolution, and where the violent overthrow of the bourgeoisie lays the foundation for the sway of the proletariat. . . .

We have seen above that the first step in the revolution by the working class is to raise [literally "promote"] the proletariat to the position of ruling class, to establish democracy.

The proletariat will use its political supremacy to wrest by degrees all capital from the bourgeoisie, to centralise all instruments of production in the hands of the state, *i.e.*, of the proletariat organised as the ruling class; and to increase the total of productive forces as rapidly as possible.**

* Karl Marx, *Poverty of Philosophy*, London and New York, 1933.—*Ed.*
** Karl Marx and Friedrich Engels, *Manifesto of the Communist Party*, Authorised English Translation of 1888, London and New York, 1932, pp. 20-30.—*Ed.*

Here we have a formulation of one of the most remarkable and most important ideas of Marxism on the subject of the state, namely, the idea of the "dictatorship of the proletariat" (as Marx and Engels began to term it after the Paris Commune) ; and also a definition of the state, in the highest degree interesting, but nevertheless also belonging to the category of "forgotten words" of Marxism: *"the state, i.e., the proletariat organised as the ruling class."*

This definition of the state, far from having ever been explained in the current propaganda and agitation literature of the official Social-Democratic parties, has been actually forgotten, as it is absolutely irreconcilable with reformism, and is a slap in the face of the common opportunist prejudices and philistine illusions about the "peaceful development of democracy."

The proletariat needs the state—this is repeated by all the opportunists, social-chauvinists and Kautskyists, who assure us that this is what Marx taught. They "forget," however, to add that, in the first place, the proletariat, according to Marx, needs only a state which is withering away, *i.e.*, a state which is so constituted that it begins to wither away immediately, and cannot but wither away; and, secondly, the workers need "a state, *i.e.*, the proletariat organised as the ruling class."

The state is a special organisation of force; it is the organisation of violence for the suppression of some class. What class must the proletariat suppress? Naturally, the exploiting class only, *i.e.*, the bourgeoisie. The toilers need the state only to overcome the resistance of the exploiters, and only the proletariat can direct this suppression and bring it to fulfilment, for the proletariat is the only class that is thoroughly revolutionary, the only class that can unite all the toilers and the exploited in the struggle against the bourgeoisie, in completely displacing it.

The exploiting classes need political rule in order to maintain exploitation, *i.e.*, in the selfish interests of an insignificant minority, and against the vast majority of the people. The exploited classes need political rule in order completely to abolish all exploitation, *i.e.*, in the interests of the vast majority of the people, and against the insignificant minority consisting of the slave-owners of modern times—the landowners and the capitalists.

The petty-bourgeois democrats, these sham Socialists who have substituted for the class struggle dreams of harmony between classes, imagined even the transition to Socialism in a dreamy fashion—not

in the form of the overthrow of the rule of the exploiting
in the form of the peaceful submission of the minority to
conscious of its aims. This petty-bourgeois Utopia, i
connected with the idea of the state's being above classes,
led to the betrayal of the interests of the toiling classes, as was
shown, for example, in the history of the French revolutions of 1848
and 1871, and in the participation of "Socialists" in bourgeois cabi-
nets in England, France, Italy and other countries at the end of the
nineteenth and the beginning of the twentieth centuries.

Marx fought all his life against this petty-bourgeois Socialism—
now reborn in Russia in the Socialist-Revolutionary and Menshevik
Parties. He carried his analysis of the class struggle logically right
to the doctrine of political power, the doctrine of the state.

The overthrow of bourgeois rule can be accomplished only by the
proletariat, as the particular class, which, by the economic conditions
of its existence, is being prepared for this work and is provided
both with the opportunity and the power to perform it. While the
capitalist class breaks up and atomises the peasantry and all the
petty-bourgeois strata, it welds together, unites and organises the
town proletariat. Only the proletariat—by virtue of its economic
rôle in large-scale production—is capable of leading *all* the toiling
and exploited masses, who are exploited, oppressed, crushed by the
bourgeoisie not less, and often more, than the proletariat, but who
are incapable of carrying on the struggle for their freedom *independently*.

The doctrine of the class struggle, as applied by Marx to the question of the state and of the Socialist revolution, leads inevitably to
the recognition of the *political rule* of the proletariat, of its dictatorship, *i.e.*, of a power shared with none and relying directly upon the
armed force of the masses. The overthrow of the bourgeoisie is
realisable only by the transformation of the proletariat into the
ruling class, able to crush the inevitable and desperate resistance of
the bourgeoisie, and to organise, for the new economic order, *all*
the toiling and exploited masses.

The proletariat needs state power, the centralised organisation of
force, the organisation of violence, both for the purpose of crushing
the resistance of the exploiters and for the purpose of *guiding* the
great mass of the population—the peasantry, the petty-bourgeoisie,
the semi-proletarians—in the work of organising Socialist economy.

By educating a workers' party, Marxism educates the vanguard the proletariat, capable of assuming power and of *leading the whole people* to Socialism, of directing and organising the new order, of being the teacher, guide and leader of all the toiling and exploited in the task of building up their social life without the bourgeoisie and against the bourgeoisie. As against this, the opportunism predominant at present breeds in the workers' party representatives of the better-paid workers, who lose touch with the rank and file, "get along" fairly well under capitalism, and sell their birthright for a mess of pottage, *i.e.*, renounce their rôle of revolutionary leaders of the people against the bourgeoisie.

"The state, *i.e.*, the proletariat organised as the ruling class"—this theory of Marx's is indissolubly connected with all his teaching concerning the revolutionary rôle of the proletariat in history. The culmination of this rôle is proletarian dictatorship, the political rule of the proletariat.

But, if the proletariat needs the state, as a *special* form of organisation of violence *against* the capitalist class, the following question arises almost automatically: is it thinkable that such an organisation can be created without a preliminary break-up and destruction of the state machinery created for *its own* use by the bourgeoisie? The *Communist Manifesto* leads straight to this conclusion, and it is of this conclusion that Marx speaks when summing up the experience of the revolution of 1848-1851.

2. Results of the Revolution

On the question of the state which we are concerned with, Marx sums up his conclusions from the revolution of 1848-1851 in the following observations contained in his work, *The Eighteenth Brumaire of Louis Bonaparte:*

> . . . But the revolution is thorough. It is still on its way through purgatory. It is completing its task methodically. By December 2nd, 1851 [the day of Louis Bonaparte's *coup d'état*], it had completed one-half of its preparatory work; now it is completing the other half. First, it perfected parliamentary power, so that it could overthrow it. Now, when it has achieved this, it is perfecting *executive power*, reducing it to its purest terms, isolating it, setting it over against itself as the sole object of reproach, so that it can *concentrate against it all its forces of destruction* [the italics are ours]. And when it has completed this second half of its preparatory work, Europe will leap to its feet and shout with joy: well grubbed, old mole!
>
> This executive power with its huge bureaucratic and military organisation, with its extensive and artificial state machinery, a horde of half a million offi-

cials in addition to an army of another half a million, this frightful body of parasites wound like a caul about the body of French society and clogging its every pore, arose in the time of the absolute monarchy in the period of the fall of feudalism, which it helped to hasten.

The first French Revolution developed centralisation,

but at the same time it developed the scope, the attributes and the servants of the government power. Napoleon perfected this state machinery. The legitimate monarchy and the July monarchy added nothing to it but a greater division of labour. . . .

Finally, in its struggle against the revolution, the parliamentary Republic found itself compelled to strengthen with its repressive measures, the resources and the centralisation of the government power. *All revolutions brought this machine to greater perfection, instead of breaking it up* [the italics are ours]. The parties which alternately contended for supremacy looked on the capture of this vast state edifice as the chief spoils of the victor.*

In this remarkable passage Marxism makes a tremendous step forward in comparison with the position of the *Communist Manifesto.* There the question of the state still is treated extremely in the abstract, in the most general terms and expressions. Here the question is treated in a concrete manner, and the conclusion is most precise, definite, practical and palpable: all revolutions which have taken place up to the present have helped to perfect the state machinery, whereas it must be shattered, broken to pieces.

This conclusion is the chief and fundamental thesis in the Marxist theory of the state. Yet it is this fundamental thesis which has been not only completely *forgotten* by the dominant official Social-Democratic parties, but directly *distorted* (as we shall see later) by the foremost theoretician of the Second International, K. Kautsky.

In the *Communist Manifesto* are summed up the general lessons of history, which force us to see in the state the organ of class domination, and lead us to the inevitable conclusion that the proletariat cannot overthrow the bourgeoisie without first conquering political power, without obtaining political rule, without transforming the state into the "proletariat organised as the ruling class"; and that this proletarian state will begin to wither away immediately after its victory, because in a society without class antagonisms, the state is unnecessary and impossible. The question as to how, from the point of view of historical development, this replacement of the capitalist state by the proletarian state shall take place, is not raised here.

* Karl Marx, *The Eighteenth Brumaire of Louis Bonaparte,* London and New York, 1933.—*Ed.*

25

It is precisely this question that Marx raises and solves in 1852. True to his philosophy of dialectical materialism, Marx takes as his basis the experience of the great revolutionary years 1848-1851. Here, as everywhere, his teaching is the *summing up of experience,* illuminated by a profound philosophical world-conception and a rich knowledge of history.

The problem of the state is put concretely: how did the bourgeois state, the state machinery necessary for the rule of the bourgeoisie, come into being? What were its changes, what its evolution in the course of the bourgeois revolutions and in the face of the independent actions of the oppressed classes? What are the tasks of the proletariat relative to this state machinery?

The centralised state power peculiar to bourgeois society came into being in the period of the fall of absolutism. Two institutions are especially characteristic of this state machinery: bureaucracy and the standing army. In their works, Marx and Engels mention repeatedly the thousand threads which connect these institutions with the bourgeoisie. The experience of every worker illustrates this connection in the clearest and most impressive manner. From its own bitter experience, the working class learns to recognise this connection; that is why it so easily acquires, so completely absorbs the doctrine revealing this inevitable connection, a doctrine which the petty-bourgeois democrats either ignorantly and light-heartedly deny, or, still more light-heartedly, admit "in general," forgetting to draw adequate practical conclusions.

Bureaucracy and the standing army constitute a "parasite" on the body of bourgeois society—a parasite born of the internal antagonisms which tear that society asunder, but essentially a parasite, "clogging every pore" of existence. The Kautskyist opportunism prevalent at present within official Social-Democracy considers this view of the state as a *parasitic organism* to be the peculiar and exclusive property of Anarchism. Naturally, this distortion of Marxism is extremely useful to those philistines who have brought Socialism to the unheard-of disgrace of justifying and embellishing the imperialist war by applying to it the term of "national defence"; but none the less it is an absolute distortion.

The development, perfecting and strengthening of the bureaucratic and military apparatus has been going on through all the bourgeois revolutions of which Europe has seen so many since the fall of feudalism. It is particularly the petty bourgeoisie that is attracted to the side of the big bourgeoisie and to its allegiance, largely by means of this apparatus, which provides the upper strata of the peasantry, small artisans and tradesmen with a number of comparatively comfortable, quiet and respectable berths raising their holders *above* the people. Consider what happened in Russia during the six months following March 12, 1917. The government posts which hitherto had been given by preference to members of the Black Hundreds now became the booty of Cadets, Mensheviks and S.-R.'s. Nobody really thought of any serious reform. They were to be put off "until the Constituent Assembly," which, in its turn, was eventually to be put off until the end of the war! But there was no delay, no waiting for a Constituent Assembly in the matter of dividing the spoils, of getting hold of the berths of Ministers, Assistant-Ministers, governor-generals, etc., etc.! The game that went on of changing the combination of persons forming the Provisional Government was, in essence, only the expression of this division and re-division of the "spoils," which was going on high and low, throughout the country, throughout the central and local government. The practical results of the six months between March 12 and September 9, 1917, beyond all dispute, are: reforms shelved, distribution of officials' berths accomplished, and "mistakes" in the distribution corrected by a few re-distributions.

But the longer the process of "re-apportioning" the bureaucratic apparatus among the various bourgeois and petty-bourgeois parties (among the Cadets, S.-R.'s and Mensheviks, if we take the case of Russia) goes on, the more clearly the oppressed classes, with the proletariat at their head, realise that they are irreconcilably hostile to the *whole* of bourgeois society. Hence the necessity for all bourgeois parties, even for the most democratic and "revolutionary-democratic" among them, to increase their repressive measures against the revolutionary proletariat, to strengthen the apparatus of repression, *i.e.*, the same state machinery. Such a course of events compels the revolution *"to concentrate all its forces of destruction"* against the state power, and to regard the problem as one, not of perfecting the machinery of the state, but of *breaking up and annihilating it.*

It was not logical theorising, but the actual course of events, the living experience of 1848-1851, that produced such a statement of the problem. To what extent Marx held strictly to the solid ground of historical experience we can see from the fact that, in 1852, he did not as yet deal concretely with the question of *what* was to replace this state machinery that was to be destroyed. Experience had not yet yielded material for the solution of this problem which history placed on the order of the day later on, in 1871. What could be laid down in 1852 with the accuracy of observation characterising the natural sciences, was that the proletarian revolution *had approached* the task of "concentrating all its forces of destruction" against the state, of "breaking up" the governmental machinery.

Here the question may arise: is it correct to generalise the experience, observations and conclusions of Marx, to apply them to a wider field than the history of France during the three years 1848-1851? To analyse this question, let us recall, first of all, a certain remark of Engels, and then proceed to examine the facts.

France—wrote Engels in his introduction to the third edition of the *Eighteenth Brumaire*—is the country where, more than anywhere else, historical class struggles have been always fought through to a decisive conclusion, and therefore where also the changing political forms within which the struggles developed, and in which their results were summed up, were stamped in sharpest outline. The centre of feudalism in the Middle Ages, the model country (since the Renaissance) of a rigidly unified monarchy, in the great revolution France shattered feudalism and established the unadulterated rule of the bourgeoisie in a more classical form than any other European country. And here also the struggle of the rising proletariat against the ruling bourgeoisie appeared in an acute form such as was unknown elsewhere.*

The last sentence is out of date, inasmuch as there has been a lull in the revolutionary struggle of the French proletariat since 1871; though, long as this lull may be, it in no way excludes the possibility that, in the coming proletarian revolution, France may once more reveal itself as the traditional home of the struggle of classes to a finish.

Let us, however, cast a general glance over the history of the more advanced countries during the end of the nineteenth and beginning of the twentieth centuries. We shall see that the same process has been going on more slowly, in more varied forms, on a much wider field: on the one hand, a development of "parliamentary power," not only in the republican countries (France, America, Switzerland), but also in the monarchies (England, Germany to a certain extent, Italy, the Scandinavian countries, etc.); on the other hand, a struggle for power of various bourgeois and petty-bourgeois parties distributing and redistributing the "spoils" of officials' berths, the founda-

* *Ibid.—Ed.*

tions of capitalist society remaining all the while unchanged; finally, the perfecting and strengthening of the "executive power," its bureaucratic and military apparatus.

There is no doubt that these are the features common to the latest stage in the evolution of all capitalist states generally. In the three years, 1848-1851, France showed, in a swift, sharp, concentrated form, all those processes of development which are inherent in the whole capitalist world.

Imperialism in particular—the era of banking capital, the era of gigantic capitalist monopolies, the era of the transformation of monopoly capitalism into state monopoly-capitalism—shows an unprecedented strengthening of the "state machinery" and an unprecedented growth of its bureaucratic and military apparatus, side by side with the increase of repressive measures against the proletariat, alike in the monarchical and the freest republican countries.

At the present time, world history is undoubtedly leading, on an incomparably larger scale than in 1852, to the "concentration of all the forces" of the proletarian revolution for the purpose of "destroying" the state machinery.

As to what the proletariat will put in its place, instructive data on the subject were furnished by the Paris Commune.

3. THE FORMULATION OF THE QUESTION BY MARX IN 1852 *

In 1907 Mehring published in the magazine *Neue Zeit* (Vol. XXV, 2, p. 164) extracts from a letter by Marx to Weydemeyer dated March 5, 1852. In this letter, among other things, is the following noteworthy observation:

As far as I am concerned, the honour does not belong to me for having discovered the existence either of classes in modern society or of the struggle between the classes. Bourgeois historians a long time before me expounded the historical development of this class struggle, and bourgeois economists, the economic anatomy of classes. What was new on my part, was to prove the following: (1) that the existence of classes is connected only with certain historical struggles which arise out of the development of production [*historische Entwicklungskämpfe der Produktion*]; (2) that class struggle necessarily leads to the dictatorship of the proletariat; (3) that this dictatorship is itself only a transition to the abolition of all classes and to a classless society.

In these words Marx has succeeded in expressing with striking clearness, first, the chief and concrete differences between his teach-

* This section was added by Lenin in the second Russian edition of *State and Revolution*, 1918.—*Ed.*

ings and those of the most advanced and profound thinkers of the bourgeoisie, and second, the essence of his teachings concerning the state.

The main point in the teaching of Marx is the class struggle. This has very often been said and written. But this is not true. Out of this error, here and there, springs an opportunist distortion of Marxism, such a falsification of it as to make it acceptable to the bourgeoisie. The theory of the class struggle was *not* created by Marx, but by the bourgeoisie *before* Marx and is, generally speaking, *acceptable* to the bourgeoisie. He who recognises *only* the class struggle is not yet a Marxist; he may be found not to have gone beyond the boundaries of bourgeois reasoning and politics. To limit Marxism to the teaching of the class struggle means to curtail Marxism—to distort it, to reduce it to something which is acceptable to the bourgeoisie. A Marxist is one who *extends* the acceptance of class struggle to the acceptance of the *dictatorship of the proletariat.* Herein lies the deepest difference between a Marxist and an ordinary petty or big bourgeois. On this touchstone it is necessary to test a *real* understanding and acceptance of Marxism. And it is not astonishing that, when the history of Europe put before the working class this question in a practical way, not only all opportunists and reformists but all Kautskyists (people who vacillate between reformism and Marxism) turned out to be miserable philistines and petty-bourgeois democrats, *denying* the dictatorship of the proletariat. Kautsky's pamphlet, *Dictatorship of the Proletariat,* published in August, 1918, *i.e.,* long after the first edition of this book, is an example of petty-bourgeois distortion of Marxism and base renunciation of it *in practice,* while hypocritically recognising it *in words* (see my pamphlet, *The Proletarian Revolution and the Renegade Kautsky,* Petrograd and Moscow, 1918).*

The present-day opportunism in the person of its main representative, the former Marxist, K. Kautsky, comes wholly under Marx's characterisation of the *bourgeois* position as quoted above, for this opportunism limits the field of recognition of the class struggle to the realm of bourgeois relationships. (Within this realm, inside of its framework, not a single educated liberal will refuse to recognise the class struggle "in principle"!) Opportunism *does not lead* the recognition of class struggle up to the main point, up to the period of *transition* from capitalism to Communism, up to the period

* See *Collected Works,* Volume XXIII.—*Ed.*

of *overthrowing* and completely abolishing the bourgeoisie. In reality, this period inevitably becomes a period of unusually violent class struggles in their sharpest possible forms and, therefore, the state during this period inevitably must be a state that is democratic *in a new way* (for the proletariat and the poor in general) and dictatorial *in a new way* (against the bourgeoisie).

Further, the substance of the teachings of Marx about the state is assimilated only by one who understands that the dictatorship of a *single* class is necessary not only for any class society generally, not only for the *proletariat* which has overthrown the bourgeoisie, but for the entire *historic period* which separates capitalism from "classless society," from Communism. The forms of bourgeois states are exceedingly variegated, but their essence is the same: in one way or another, all these states are in the last analysis inevitably a *dictatorship of the bourgeoisie*. The transition from capitalism to Communism will certainly bring a great variety and abundance of political forms, but the essence will inevitably be only one: *the dictatorship of the proletariat*.

CHAPTER III

EXPERIENCE OF THE PARIS COMMUNE OF 1871: MARX'S ANALYSIS

1. IN WHAT DOES THE HEROISM OF THE COMMUNARDS CONSIST?

IT is well known that in the autumn of 1870, a few months prior to the Commune, Marx warned the Paris workers that an attempt to overthrow the government would be the folly of despair. But when, in March, 1871, a decisive battle was *forced* upon the workers and they accepted it, when the uprising had become a fact, Marx welcomed the proletarian revolution with the greatest enthusiasm, in spite of unfavourable auguries. Marx did not assume the rigid attitude of pedantically condemning an "untimely" movement as did the ill-famed Russian renegade from Marxism, Plekhanov, who, in November, 1905, wrote encouragingly about the workers' and peasants' struggle but, after December, 1905, cried, liberal fashion: "They should not have taken up arms." [4]

Marx, however, was not only enthusiastic about the heroism of the Communards who "stormed the heavens," as he expressed himself. He saw in the mass revolutionary movement, although it did not attain its aim, an historic experiment of gigantic importance, a certain advance of the world proletarian revolution, a practical step more important than hundreds of programmes and discussions. To analyse this experiment, to draw from it lessons in tactics, to reexamine his theory in the new light it afforded—such was the problem as it presented itself to Marx.

The only "correction" which Marx thought it necessary to make in the *Communist Manifesto* was made by him on the basis of the revolutionary experience of the Paris Communards.

The last preface to a new German edition of the *Communist Manifesto* signed by both its authors is dated June 24, 1872. In this preface the authors, Karl Marx and Friedrich Engels, say that the programme of the *Communist Manifesto* is now "in places out of date."

One thing especially—they continue—was proved by the Commune, viz., that the "working class cannot simply lay hold of the ready-made state machinery and wield it for its own purposes." *

The words within quotation marks in this passage are borrowed by its authors from Marx's book, *The Civil War in France.*

It thus appears that one principal and fundamental lesson of the Paris Commune was considered by Marx and Engels to be of such enormous importance that they introduced it as a vital correction into the *Communist Manifesto.*

It is most characteristic that it is precisely this vital correction which has been distorted by the opportunists, and its meaning, probably, is not known to nine-tenths, if not ninety-nine-hundredths, of the readers of the *Communist Manifesto.* We shall deal with this distortion more fully further on, in a chapter devoted specially to distortions. It will be sufficient here to note that the current vulgar "interpretation" of Marx's famous utterance quoted above consists in asserting that Marx is here emphasising the idea of gradual development, in contradistinction to a seizure of power, and so on.

As a matter of fact, *exactly the opposite is the case.* Marx's idea is that the working class must *break up, shatter* the "ready-made state machinery," and not confine itself merely to taking possession of it.

On April 12, 1871, *i.e.,* just at the time of the Commune, Marx wrote to Kugelmann:

If you look at the last chapter of my *Eighteenth Brumaire,* you will see that I declare that the next attempt of the French Revolution must be: not, as in the past, to transfer the bureaucratic and military machinery from one hand to the other, but to *break it up* [Marx's italics—the original is *zerbrechen*]; and this is the precondition of any real people's revolution on the Continent. And this is what our heroic party comrades in Paris have attempted.**

In these words, "to break up the bureaucratic and military machinery," is contained, briefly formulated, the principal lesson of Marxism on the tasks of the proletariat in relation to the state during a revolution. And it is just this lesson which has not only been

---

* Karl Marx and Friedrich Engels, *Manifesto of the Communist Party,* London and New York, 1932, p. 7.—*Ed.*

** *Neue Zeit,* XX-1, 1901-1902, p. 709. The letters from Marx to Kugelmann have come out in Russian in no less than two editions, one of them edited and with an introduction by me. [Karl Marx, *Letters to Kugelmann,* London and New York, 1933.—*Ed.*].

forgotten, but downright distorted, by the prevailing Kautskyist "interpretation" of Marxism.

As for Marx's reference to the *Eighteenth Brumaire,* we have quoted above the corresponding passage in full.

It is interesting to note two particular points in the passages of Marx quoted. First, he confines his conclusions to the Continent. This was natural in 1871, when England was still the model of a purely capitalist country, but without a military machine and, in large measure, without a bureaucracy. Hence Marx excluded England, where a revolution, even a people's revolution, could be imagined, and was then possible, *without* the preliminary condition of destroying the "ready-made state machinery."

Today, in 1917, in the epoch of the first great imperialist war, this exception made by Marx is no longer valid. Both England and America, the greatest and last representatives of Anglo-Saxon "liberty" in the sense of the absence of militarism and bureaucracy, have today plunged headlong into the all-European dirty, bloody morass of military bureaucratic institutions to which everything is subordinated and which trample everything under foot. Today, both in England and in America, the "precondition of any real people's revolution" is the *break-up,* the *shattering* of the "ready-made state machinery" (brought in those countries, between 1914 and 1917, to general "European" imperialist perfection).

Secondly, particular attention should be given to Marx's extremely profound remark that the destruction of the military and bureaucratic apparatus of the state is "the precondition of any real *people's* revolution." This idea of a "people's" revolution seems strange on Marx's lips, and the Russian Plekhanovists and Mensheviks, those followers of Struve who wish to be considered Marxists, might possibly declare such an expression to be a "slip of the tongue." They have reduced Marxism to such a state of poverty-stricken "liberal" distortion that nothing exists for them beyond the distinction between bourgeois and proletarian revolution—and even that distinction they understand in an entirely lifeless way.

If we take for examples the revolutions of the twentieth century, we shall, of course, have to recognise both the Portuguese and the Turkish revolutions as bourgeois. Neither, however, is a "people's" revolution, inasmuch as the mass of the people, the enormous majority, does not make its appearance actively, independently, with its own economic and political demands, in either the one or the other.

On the other hand, the Russian bourgeois revolution of 1905-1907, although it presented no such "brilliant" successes as at times fell to the lot of the Portuguese and Turkish revolutions, was undoubtedly a real "people's" revolution, since the mass of the people, the majority, the lowest social "depths," crushed down by oppression and exploitation, were rising independently, since they put on the entire course of the revolution the stamp of *their* demands, *their* attempts at building up, in their own way, a new society in place of the old society that was being shattered.

In the Europe of 1871, the proletariat on the Continent did not constitute the majority of the people. A "people's" revolution, actually sweeping the majority into its current, could be such only if it embraced both the proletariat and the peasantry. Both classes then constituted the "people." Both classes are united by the circumstance that the "bureaucratic and military state machinery" oppresses, crushes, exploits them. To *shatter* this machinery, to *break it up*—this is the true interest of the "people," of its majority, the workers and most of the peasants, this is the "preliminary condition" of a free union of the poorest peasantry with the proletarians; while, without such a union, democracy is unstable and Socialist reorganisation is impossible.

Towards such a union, as is well known, the Paris Commune was making its way, though it did not reach its goal, owing to a number of circumstances, internal and external.

Consequently, when speaking of "a real people's revolution," Marx, without in the least forgetting the peculiar characteristics of the petty bourgeoisie (he spoke of them much and often), was very carefully taking into account the actual interrelation of classes in most of the continental European states in 1871. On the other hand, he stated that the "breaking up" of the state machinery is demanded by the interests both of the workers and of the peasants, that it unites them, that it places before them the common task of removing the "parasite" and replacing it by something new.

By what exactly?

2. What Is to Replace the Shattered State Machinery?

In 1847, in the *Communist Manifesto*, Marx answered this question still in a purely abstract manner, stating the problems rather than the methods of solving them. To replace this machinery by "the proletariat organised as the ruling class," by "establishing democracy"—such was the answer of the *Communist Manifesto*.

Without resorting to Utopias, Marx waited for the *experience* of a mass movement to produce the answer to the problem as to the exact forms which this organisation of the proletariat as the ruling class will assume and as to the exact manner in which this organisation will be combined with the most complete, most consistent "establishment of democracy."

The experiment of the Commune, meagre as it was, was subjected by Marx to the most careful analysis in his *The Civil War in France*. Let us quote the most important passages of this work.

There developed in the nineteenth century, he says, originating from the days of absolute monarchy, "the centralised state power, with its ubiquitous organs of standing army, police, bureaucracy, clergy and judicature." With the development of class antagonism between capital and labour, "the state power assumed more and more the character of the national power of capital over labour, of a public force organised for social enslavement, of an engine of class despotism. After every revolution marking a progressive phase in the class struggle, the purely repressive character of the state power stands out in bolder and bolder relief." The state power, after the revolution of 1848-1849 became "the national war engine of capital against labour." The Second Empire consolidated this.

"The direct antithesis of the Empire was the Commune," says Marx. It was the "positive form" of "a republic that was not only to supersede the monarchical form of class rule, but class rule itself."

What was this "positive" form of the proletarian, the Socialist republic? What was the state it was beginning to create?

"The first decree of the Commune . . . was the suppression of the standing army, and the substitution for it of the armed people," says Marx.*

This demand now figures in the programme of every party calling itself Socialist. But the value of their programmes is best shown by the behaviour of our Socialist-Revolutionaries and Mensheviks, who, even after the revolution of March 12, 1917, refused to carry out this demand in practice!

The Commune was formed of municipal councillors, chosen by universal suffrage in various wards of the town, responsible and revocable at short terms. The majority of its members were naturally working men, or acknowledged rep-

* Karl Marx, *The Civil War in France*, London and New York, 1933.—*Ed.*

resentatives of the working class. . . . Instead of continuing to b
of the Central Government, the police was at once stripped of its
tributes, and turned into the responsible and at all times revocable ɩ
Commune. So were the officials of all other branches of the adn
From the members of the Commune downwards, the public service
done at *workmen's wages*. The vested interests and the representa
ances of the high dignitaries of state disappeared along with the high
themselves. . . .

Having once got rid of the standing army and the police, the physical force
elements of the old government, the Commune was anxious to break the
spiritual force of repression, the "parson power." . . .

The judicial functionaries were to be divested of [their] sham independence.
. . . Like the rest of public servants, magistrates and judges were to be elective,
responsible and revocable.*

Thus the Commune would appear to have replaced the shattered
state machinery "only" by fuller democracy: abolition of the standing army; all officials to be fully elective and subject to recall. But,
as a matter of fact this "only" signifies a gigantic replacement of one
type of institution by others of a fundamentally different order.
Here we observe a case of "transformation of quantity into quality":
democracy, introduced as fully and consistently as is generally thinkable, is transformed from capitalist democracy into proletarian democracy; from the state (*i.e.*, a special force for the suppression of a
particular class) into something which is no longer really the state
in the accepted sense of the word.

It is still necessary to suppress the bourgeoisie and crush its resistance. This was particularly necessary for the Commune; and
one of the reasons of its defeat was that it did not do this with sufficient determination. But the organ of suppression is now the
majority of the population, and not a minority, as was always the
case under slavery, serfdom, and wage labour. And, once the majority of the people *itself* suppresses its oppressors, a "special force"
for suppression is *no longer necessary.* In this sense the state *begins
to wither away*. Instead of the special institutions of a privileged
minority (privileged officialdom, heads of a standing army), the
majority can itself directly fulfil all these functions; and the more
the discharge of the functions of state power devolves upon the
people generally, the less need is there for the existence of this
power.

In this connection the Commune's measure emphasised by Marx,
particularly worthy of note, is: the abolition of all representation
allowances, and of all money privileges in the case of officials, the

* *Ibid.—Ed.*

37

reduction of the remuneration of *all* servants of the state to *"work-ingmen's wages."* Here is shown, more clearly than anywhere else, the *break* from a bourgeois democracy to a proletarian democracy, from the democracy of the oppressors to the democracy of the oppressed classes, from the state as a "special force for suppression" of a given class to the suppression of the oppressors by the *whole force* of the majority of the people—the workers and the peasants. And it is precisely on this most striking point, perhaps the most important as far as the problem of the state is concerned, that the teachings of Marx have been entirely forgotten! In popular commentaries, whose number is legion, this is not mentioned. It is "proper" to keep silent about it as if it were a piece of old-fashioned "naïveté," just as the Christians, after Christianity had attained the position of a state religion, "forgot" the "naïvetés" of primitive Christianity with its democratic-revolutionary spirit.

The reduction of the remuneration of the highest state officials seems "simply" a demand of naïve, primitive democracy. One of the "founders" of modern opportunism, the former Social-Democrat, Eduard Bernstein, has more than once exercised his talents in repeating the vulgar bourgeois jeers at "primitive" democracy. Like all opportunists, including the present Kautskyists, he fails completely to understand that, first of all, the transition from capitalism to Socialism is *impossible* without "return," in a measure, to "primitive" democracy (how can one otherwise pass on to the discharge of all the state functions by the majority of the population and by every individual of the population?); and, secondly, he forgets that "primitive democracy" on the basis of capitalism and capitalist culture is not the same primitive democracy as in prehistoric or pre-capitalist times. Capitalist culture has *created* large-scale production, factories, railways, the postal service, telephones, etc., and *on this basis* the great majority of functions of the old "state power" have become so simplified and can be reduced to such simple operations of registration, filing and checking that they will be quite within the reach of every literate person, and it will be possible to perform them for "workingmen's wages," which circumstance can (and must) strip those functions of every shadow of privilege, of every appearance of "official grandeur."

All officials, without exception, elected and subject to recall *at any time*, their salaries reduced to "workingmen's wages"—these simple and "self-evident" democratic measures, which, completely uniting the interests of the workers and the majority of peasants, at the same time serve as a bridge leading from capitalism to Socialism. These measures refer to the state, to the purely political reconstruction of society; but, of course, they acquire their full meaning and significance only in connection with the "expropriation of the expropriators," either accomplished or in preparation, *i.e.*, with the turning of capitalist private ownership of the means of production into social ownership. Marx wrote:

> The Commune made that catchword of bourgeois revolutions, cheap government, a reality by destroying the two greatest sources of expenditure—the standing army and state functionarism.*

From the peasantry, as from other sections of the petty bourgeoisie, only an insignificant few "rise to the top," occupy "a place in the sun" in the bourgeois sense, *i.e.*, become either well-to-do people or secure and privileged officials. The great majority of peasants in every capitalist country where the peasantry exists (and the majority of capitalist countries are of this kind) is oppressed by the government and longs for its overthrow, longs for "cheap" government. This can be realised *only* by the proletariat; and by realising it, the proletariat makes at the same time a step forward towards the Socialist reconstruction of the state.

3. THE DESTRUCTION OF PARLIAMENTARISM

> The Commune—says Marx—was to be a working, not a parliamentary body, executive and legislative at the same time. . . .
> Instead of deciding once in three or six years which member of the ruling class was to represent the people in Parliament, universal suffrage was to serve the people, constituted in Communes, as individual suffrage serves every other employer in the search for the workmen and managers in his business.**

This remarkable criticism of parliamentarism made in 1871 also belongs to the "forgotten words" of Marxism, thanks to the prevalence of social-chauvinism and opportunism. Ministers and professional parliamentarians, traitors to the proletariat and Socialist "sharks" of our day, have left all criticism of parliamentarism to the Anarchists, and, on this wonderfully intelligent ground, denounce *all* criticism of parliamentarism as "Anarchism"!! It is not surprising that the proletariat of the most "advanced" parliamentary countries, being disgusted with such "Socialists" as Messrs. Scheide-

* *Ibid.—Ed.*   ** *Ibid.—Ed.*

mann, David, Legien, Sembat, Renaudel Henderson, Vandervelde, Stauning, Branting, Bissolati and Co. has been giving its sympathies more and more to Anarcho-syndicalism, in spite of the fact that it is but the twin brother of opportunism.

But to Marx, revolutionary dialectics was never the empty fashion-able phrase, the toy rattle, which Plekhanov, Kautsky and the others have made of it. Marx knew how to break with Anarchism ruth-lessly for its inability to make use of the "stable" of bourgeois par-liamentarism, especially at a time when the situation was not revo-lutionary; but at the same time he knew how to subject parliamen-tarism to a really revolutionary-proletarian criticism.

To decide once every few years which member of the ruling class is to repress and oppress the people through parliament—this is the real essence of bourgeois parliamentarism, not only in parliamentary-constitutional monarchies, but also in the most democratic republics.

But, if the question of the state is raised, if parliamentarism is to be regarded as one institution of the state, what then, from the point of view of the tasks of the proletariat in *this* realm, is to be the way out of parliamentarism? How can we do without it?

Again and again we must repeat: the teaching of Marx, based on the study of the Commune, has been so completely forgotten that any criticism of parliamentarism other than Anarchist or reactionary is quite unintelligible to a present-day "Social-Democrat" (read: present-day traitor to Socialism).

The way out of parliamentarism is to be found, of course, not in the abolition of the representative institutions and the elective prin-ciple, but in the conversion of the representative institutions from mere "talking shops" into working bodies. "The Commune was to be a working, not a parliamentary body, executive and legislative at the same time."

"A working, not a parliamentary body"—this hits the vital spot of present-day parliamentarians and the parliamentary Social-Demo-cratic "lap-dogs"! Take any parliamentary country, from America to Switzerland, from France to England, Norway and so forth—the actual work of the "state" there is done behind the scenes and is carried out by the departments, the offices and the staffs. Parliament itself is given up to talk for the special purpose of fooling the "common people." This is so true that even in the Russian republic, a bourgeois-democratic republic, all these aims of parliamentarism were immediately revealed, even before a real parliament was created. Such heroes of rotten philistinism as the Skobelevs and the Tseretelis, Chernovs and Avksentyevs, have managed to pollute even the Soviets, after the model of the most despicable petty-bourgeois parliamentarism, by turning them into hollow talking shops. In the Soviets, the Right Honourable "Socialist" Ministers are fooling the confiding peasants with phrase-mongering and resolutions. In the government itself a sort of permanent quadrille is going on in order that, on the one hand, as many S.-R.'s and Mensheviks as possible may get at the "gravy," the "soft" jobs, and, on the other hand, the attention of the people may be occupied. All the while the real "state" business is being done in the offices, in the staffs.

The *Dyelo Naroda,* organ of the ruling Socialist-Revolutionary Party, recently admitted in an editorial article—with the incomparable candour of people of "good society," in which "all" are engaged in political prostitution—that even in those ministries which belong to the "Socialists" (please excuse the term), the whole bureaucratic apparatus remains essentially the same as of old, working as of old, and "freely" obstructing revolutionary measures. Even if we did not have this admission, would not the actual history of the participation of the S.-R.'s and Mensheviks in the government prove this? It is only characteristic that—while in ministerial company with the Cadets—Messrs. Chernov, Rusanov, Zenzinov and other editors of the *Dyelo Naroda* have so completely lost all shame that they unblushingly proclaim, as if it were a mere bagatelle, that in "their" ministries everything remains as of old!! Revolutionary-democratic phrases to gull the Simple Simons; bureaucracy and red tape for the "benefit" of the capitalists—here you have the *essence* of the "honourable" coalition.

The venal and rotten parliamentarism of bourgeois society is replaced in the Commune by institutions in which freedom of opinion and discussion does not degenerate into deception, for the parliamentarians must themselves work, must themselves execute their own laws, must themselves verify their results in actual life, must themselves be directly responsible to their electorate. Representative institutions remain, but parliamentarism as a special system, as a division of labour between the legislative and the executive functions, as a privileged position for the deputies, *no longer exists.* Without representative institutions we cannot imagine democracy, not even proletarian democracy; but we can and *must* think of democracy without parliamentarism, if criticism of bourgeois society is not mere empty words for us, if the desire to over-throw the rule of the bourgeoisie is our serious and sincere desire, and not a mere "election cry" for catching workingmen's votes, as it is with the Mensheviks and S.-R.'s, the Scheidemanns, the Legiens, the Sembats and the Vanderveldes.

It is most instructive to notice that, in speaking of the functions of *those* officials who are necessary both in the Commune and in the proletarian democracy, Marx compares them with the workers of "every other employer," that is, of the usual capitalist concern, with its "workers and managers."

There is no trace of Utopianism in Marx, in the sense of inventing or imagining a "new" society. No, he studies, as a process of natural history, the *birth* of the new society *from* the old, the forms of transition from the latter to the former. He takes the actual experience of a mass proletarian movement and tries to draw practical lessons from it. He "learns" from the Commune, as all great revolutionary thinkers have not been afraid to learn from the experience of great movements of the oppressed classes, never preaching them pedantic "sermons" (such as Plekhanov's: "They should not have taken up arms"; or Tsereteli's: "A class must know how to limit itself").

To destroy officialdom immediately, everywhere, completely—this cannot be thought of. That is a Utopia. But to *break up* at once the old bureaucratic machine and to start immediately the construction of a new one which will enable us gradually to reduce all officialdom to naught—this is *no* Utopia, it is the experience of the Commune, it is the direct and urgent task of the revolutionary proletariat.

Capitalism simplifies the functions of "state" administration; it makes it possible to throw off "commanding" methods and to reduce everything to a matter of the organisation of the proletarians (as the ruling class), hiring "workmen and managers" in the name of the whole of society.

We are not Utopians, we do not indulge in "dreams" of how best to do away *immediately* with all administration, with all subordination; these Anarchist dreams, based upon a lack of understanding of the task of proletarian dictatorship, are basically foreign to Marxism, and, as a matter of fact, they serve but to put off the Socialist revolution until human nature is different. No, we want the Socialist

revolution with human nature as it is now, with human n
cannot do without subordination, control, and "manager

But if there be subordination, it must be to the arm
of all the exploited and the labouring—to the proleta.
specific "commanding" methods of the state officials can and mu.
begin to be replaced—immediately, within twenty-four hours—by
the simple functions of "managers" and bookkeepers, functions which
are now already within the capacity of the average city dweller and
can well be performed for "workingmen's wages."

We organise large-scale production, starting from what capitalism
has already created; we workers *ourselves,* relying on our own experience as workers, establishing a strict, an iron discipline, sup-
ported by the state power of the armed workers, shall reduce the
rôle of the state officials to that of simply carrying out our instruc-
tions as responsible, moderately paid "managers" (of course, with
technical knowledge of all sorts, types and degrees). This is *our*
proletarian task, with this we can and must *begin* when carrying
through a proletarian revolution. Such a beginning, on the basis
of large-scale production, of itself leads to the gradual "withering
away" of all bureaucracy, to the gradual creation of a new order,
an order without quotation marks, an order which has nothing to do
with wage slavery, an order in which the more and more simplified
functions of control and accounting will be performed by each in
turn, will then become a habit, and will finally die out as *special*
functions of a special stratum of the population.

A witty German Social-Democrat of the 'seventies of the last century called the *post-office* an example of the socialist system. This
is very true. At present the post-office is a business organised on
the lines of a state *capitalist* monopoly. Imperialism is gradually
transforming all trusts into organisations of a similar type. Above
the "common" workers, who are overloaded with work and starving,
there stands here the same bourgeois bureaucracy. But the mechanism of social management is here already to hand. Overthrow the
capitalists, crush with the iron hand of the armed workers the
resistance of these exploiters, break the bureaucratic machine of
the modern state—and you have before you a mechanism of the
highest technical equipment, freed of "parasites," capable of being
set into motion by the united workers themselves who hire their own
technicians, managers, bookkeepers, and pay them *all*, as, indeed,
every "state" official, with the usual workers' wage. Here is a con-

rete, practicable task, immediately realisable in relation to all trusts, a task that frees the workers of exploitation and makes use of the experience (especially in the realm of the construction of the state) which the Commune began to reveal in practice.

To organise the *whole* national economy like the postal system, in such a way that the technicians, managers, bookkeepers as well as *all* officials, should receive no higher wages than "workingmen's wages," all under the control and leadership of the armed proletariat—this is our immediate aim. This is the kind of state and economic basis we need. This is what will produce the destruction of parliamentarism, while retaining representative institutions. This is what will free the labouring classes from the prostitution of these institutions by the bourgeoisie.

4. The Organisation of National Unity

In a rough sketch of national organisation which the Commune had no time to develop, it states clearly that the Commune was to be the political form of even the smallest country hamlet. . . .

From these Communes would be elected the "National Delegation" at Paris.

The few but important functions which still would remain for a central government were not to be suppressed, as has been intentionally misstated, but were to be discharged by Communal, and, therefore, strictly responsible agents. The unity of the nation was not to be broken; but, on the contrary, to be organised by the Communal constitution, and to become a reality by the destruction of the state power which claimed to be the embodiment of that unity independent of, and superior to, the nation itself, from which it was but a parasitic excrescence. While the merely repressive organs of the old governmental power were to be amputated, its legitimate functions were to be wrested from an authority usurping pre-eminence over society itself, and restored to the responsible agents of society.*

To what extent the opportunists of contemporary Social-Democracy have failed to understand—or perhaps it would be more true to say, did not want to understand—these observations of Marx is best shown by the famous (Herostrates-fashion) book of the renegade Bernstein, *Die Voraussetzungen des Sozialismus und die Aufgaben der Sozialdemokratie.** It is just in connection with the above passage from Marx that Bernstein wrote saying that this programme

* *Ibid.—Ed.*
** An English translation is published under the title *Evolutionary Socialism.—Ed.*

... in its political content displays, in all its essential features, the greatest similarity to the federalism of Proudhon. . . . In spite of all the other points of difference between Marx and the "petty-bourgeois" Proudhon [Bernstein places the words "petty-bourgeois" in quotation marks in order to make them sound ironical] on these points their ways of thinking resemble each other as closely as could be.

Of course, Bernstein continues, the importance of the municipalities is growing, but:

... it seems to me doubtful whether the first task of democracy would be such a dissolution [*Auflösung*] of the modern states and such a complete transformation [*Umwandlung*] of their organisation as is described by Marx and Proudhon (the formation of a national assembly from delegates of the provincial or district assemblies, which, in their turn, would consist of delegates from the Communes), so that the whole previous mode of national representation would vanish completely.*

This is really monstrous: thus to confuse Marx's views on the "destruction of the state power," of the "parasitic excrescence" with the federalism of Proudhon! But this is no accident, for it never occurs to the opportunist that Marx is not speaking here at all of federalism as opposed to centralism, but of the destruction of the old bourgeois state machinery which exists in all bourgeois countries.

To the opportunist occurs only what he sees around him, in a society of petty-bourgeois philistinism and "reformist" stagnation, namely, only "municipalities"! As for a proletarian revolution, the opportunist has forgotten even how to imagine it.

It is amusing. But it is remarkable that on this point nobody argued against Bernstein! Bernstein has been refuted often enough, especially by Plekhanov in Russian literature and by Kautsky in European, but neither made *any* remark upon *this* perversion of Marx by Bernstein.

To such an extent has the opportunist forgotten to think in a revolutionary way and forgotten how to reflect on revolution, that he attributes "federalism" to Marx, mixing him up with the founder of Anarchism, Proudhon. And Kautsky and Plekhanov, anxious to be orthodox Marxists and to defend the teaching of revolutionary Marxism, are silent on this point! Herein lies one of the roots of that vulgarisation of the ideas concerning the difference between Marxism and Anarchism, which is common to both Kautskyists and opportunists, and which we shall discuss later.

Federalism is not touched upon in Marx's observations about the

* Bernstein, *ibid.*, German Edition, 1899, pp. 134-136.

45

experience of the Commune, as quoted above. Marx agrees with Proudhon precisely on that point which has quite escaped the opportunist Bernstein. Marx differs from Proudhon just on the point where Bernstein sees their agreement.

Marx agrees with Proudhon in that they both stand for the "destruction" of the contemporary state machinery. This common ground of Marxism with Anarchism (both with Proudhon and with Bakunin) neither the opportunists nor the Kautskyists wish to see, for on this point they have themselves departed from Marxism.

Marx differs both from Proudhon and Bakunin precisely on the point of federalism (not to speak of the dictatorship of the proletariat). Federalism arises, as a principle, from the petty-bourgeois views of Anarchism. Marx is a centralist. In the above-quoted observations of his there is no deviation from centralism. Only people full of petty-bourgeois "superstitious faith" in the state can mistake the destruction of the bourgeois state for the destruction of centralism.

But will it not be centralism if the proletariat and poorest peasantry take the power of the state in their own hands, organise themselves freely into communes, and *unite* the action of all the communes in striking at capital, in crushing the resistance of the capitalists, in the transfer of private property in railways, factories, land, and so forth, to the *entire* nation, to the whole of society? Will that not be the most consistent democratic centralism? And proletarian centralism at that?

Bernstein simply cannot conceive the possibility of voluntary centralism, of a voluntary union of the communes into a nation, a voluntary fusion of the proletarian communes in the process of destroying bourgeois supremacy and the bourgeois state machinery. Like all philistines, Bernstein can imagine centralism only as something from above, to be imposed and maintained solely by means of bureaucracy and militarism.

Marx, as though he foresaw the possibility of the perversion of his ideas, purposely emphasises that the accusation against the Commune that it desired to destroy the unity of the nation, to do away with a central power, was a deliberate falsehood. Marx purposely uses the phrase "to organise the unity of the nation," so as to contrast conscious, democratic, proletarian centralism to bourgeois, military, bureaucratic centralism.

But no one is so deaf as he who will not hear. The opportunists of contemporary Social-Democracy do not, on any account, want to hear of destroying the state power, of cutting off the parasite.

5. DESTRUCTION OF THE PARASITE-STATE

We have already quoted part of Marx's statements on this subject, and must now complete his presentation.

It is generally the fate of completely new historical creations—wrote Marx—to be mistaken for the counterpart of older and even defunct forms of social life, to which they may bear a certain likeness. Thus, this new Commune, which breaks [bricht] the modern state power, has been mistaken for a reproduction of the mediaeval Communes . . . for a federation of small states [Montesquieu, the Girondins] . . . for an exaggerated form of the ancient struggle against over-centralisation. . . . The Communal Constitution would have restored to the social body all the forces hitherto absorbed by the state parasite feeding upon, and clogging the free movements of, society. By this one act it would have initiated the regeneration of France . . . the Communal Constitution brought the rural producers under the intellectual lead of the central towns of their districts, and there secured to them, in the working man, the natural trustees of their interests. The very existence of the Commune involved, as a matter of course, local municipal liberty, but no longer as a check upon the, now superseded, state power.*

"Breaks the modern state power," which was a "parasitic excrescence"; its "amputation," its "destruction"; "the now superseded state power"—these are the expressions used by Marx regarding the state when he appraised and analysed the experience of the Commune.

All this was written a little less than half a century ago; and now one has to undertake excavations, as it were, in order to bring uncorrupted Marxism to the knowledge of the masses. The conclusions drawn from the observation of the last great revolution, through which Marx lived, have been forgotten just at the moment when the time had arrived for the next great proletarian revolutions.

The multiplicity of interpretations to which the Commune has been subjected, and the multiplicity of interests which construed it in their favour, show that it was a thoroughly expansive political form, while all previous forms of government had been emphatically repressive. Its true secret was this. It was essentially *a working class government*, the product of the struggle of the producing against the appropriating class, the political form at last discovered under which to work out the economical emancipation of labour.

Except on this last condition, the Communal Constitution would have been an impossibility and a delusion.**

The Utopians busied themselves with the "discovery" of the political forms under which the Socialist reconstruction of society

* *The Civil War in France.—Ed.*   ** *Ibid.—Ed.*

could take place. The Anarchists turned away from the question of political forms altogether. The opportunists of modern Social-Democracy accepted the bourgeois political forms of a parliamentary, democratic state as the limit which cannot be overstepped; they broke their foreheads praying before this idol, denouncing as Anarchism every attempt to *destroy* these forms.

Marx deducted from the whole history of Socialism and political struggle that the state was bound to disappear, and that the transitional form of its disappearance (the transition from the political state to no state) would be the "proletariat organised as the ruling class." But Marx did not undertake the task of *discovering* the political *forms* of this future stage. He limited himself to an exact observation of French history, its analysis and the conclusion to which the year 1851 had led, *viz.*, that matters were moving towards the *destruction* of the bourgeois machinery of state.

And when the mass revolutionary movement of the proletariat burst forth, Marx, in spite of the failure of that movement, in spite of its short life and its patent weakness, began to study what political forms it had *disclosed*.

The Commune is the form "at last discovered" by the proletarian revolution, under which the economic liberation of labour can proceed.

The Commune is the first attempt of a proletarian revolution to *break up* the bourgeois state machinery and constitutes the political form, "at last discovered," which can and must *take the place* of the broken machine.

We shall see below that the Russian Revolutions of 1905 and 1917, in different surroundings and under different circumstances, continued the work of the Commune and confirmed the historic analysis made by the genius of Marx.

CHAPTER IV

SUPPLEMENTARY EXPLANATIONS BY ENGELS

MARX gave the fundamentals on the question of the meaning of the experience of the Commune. Engels returned to the same question repeatedly, elucidating Marx's analysis and conclusions, sometimes so forcibly throwing *other* sides of the question into relief that we must dwell on these explanations separately.

1. THE HOUSING QUESTION

In his work on the housing question (1872) Engels took into account the experience of the Commune, dwelling repeatedly on the tasks of the revolution in relation to the state. It is interesting to note that in the treatment of this concrete subject there become clear, on the one hand, the features common to the proletarian state and the present state—features which permit of speaking of a state in both cases—and, on the other hand, the features which differentiate them, or the transition to the destruction of the state.

How then is the housing question to be solved? In present-day society, it is solved as every other social question is solved: by the gradual economic equalisation of supply and demand, a solution which ever anew begets the very same question, and is consequently no solution at all. How a social revolution would solve this question depends not only on the circumstances then existing, but is also connected with much more far-reaching questions, one of the most important of which is the abolition of the antagonism between town and country. As it is not our business to make any utopian systems for the organisation of the society of the future, it would be more than idle to go into this. But this much at least is certain, that in the large towns there are already enough dwelling houses, if these were made rational use of, to immediately relieve any real "housing shortage." This, of course, can only be done by the expropriation of the present owners and by quartering in their houses workers who are homeless or are excessively overcrowded in their present quarters; and as soon as the proletariat has conquered political power, such a measure, demanded in the interests of public welfare, would be as easy to carry through as other expropriations and quarterings by the state of today.*

Here the change in the form of the state power is not considered, but only the content of its activity. Expropriations and the occupa-

* Friedrich Engels, *The Housing Question*, London and New York, 1933.—*Ed.*

49

tion of houses take place by order even of the present state. The proletarian state, from the formal point of view, will also "order" the occupation of houses and expropriation of buildings. But it is clear that the old executive apparatus, the bureaucracy connected with the bourgeoisie, would simply be unfit to carry out the orders of the proletarian state.

> . . . It must, however, be stated that the "actual seizure of possession" of all instruments of labour, the taking possession of the whole of industry by the working people, is the direct opposite of the Proudhonist "solution." In the latter, the *individual worker* becomes the owner of a house, a farm, and the instruments of labour; in the former, the "working people" remains the collective owner of the houses, factories and instruments of labour, and will hardly, at any rate during a transition period, hand over the usufruct of these to individuals or companies unless the costs are met by them. It is just the same as with the abolition of property in land, which is not the abolition of ground rent, but only its transfer, even though in modified form, to society. The actual taking possession of all instruments of labour by the working people therefore by no means excludes the retention of rent relations.*

One question touched upon here, namely, the economic reasons for the withering away of the state, we shall discuss in the next chapter. Engels expresses himself most cautiously, saying that the proletarian state will "hardly" allot houses without pay, "at any rate, during a transition period." The renting out to separate families of houses belonging to the whole people presupposes the collection of rent, a certain amount of control, and some rules underlying the allotment of houses. All this demands a certain form of state, but it does not at all demand a special military and bureaucratic apparatus, with officials occupying especially privileged positions. Transition to a state of affairs when it will be possible to let houses without rent is bound up with the complete "withering away" of the state.

Speaking of the conversion of the Blanquists, after the Commune and under the influence of its experience, to the principles of Marxism, Engels, in passing, formulates these principles as follows:

> . . . Necessity of political action by the proletariat, and its dictatorship as the transition to the abolition of classes and, with them, of the state. . . .**

Those addicted to hair-splitting criticism, and those who belong to the bourgeois "exterminators of Marxism," will perhaps see a contradiction, in the above quotation from the *Anti-Dühring*, between this *avowal* of the "abolition of the state" and the repudiation of a formula like the Anarchist one. It would not be surprising if the opportunists stamped Engels, too, as an "Anarchist," for the social-chauvinists are now more and more adopting the method of accusing the internationalists of Anarchism.

That, together with the abolition of classes, the state will also be abolished, Marxism has always taught. The well-known passage on the "withering away of the state" in the *Anti-Dühring* does not blame the Anarchists for being in favour of the abolition of the state, but for preaching that the state can be abolished "within twenty-four hours."

In view of the fact that the present predominant "Social-Democratic" doctrine completely distorts the relation of Marxism to Anarchism on the question of the abolition of the state, it will be quite useful to recall a certain polemic of Marx and Engels against the Anarchists.

2. POLEMIC AGAINST THE ANARCHISTS

This polemic took place in 1873. Marx and Engels contributed articles against the Proudhonists, "autonomists" or "anti-authoritarians," to an Italian Socialist publication, and it was not until 1913 that these articles appeared in German translation in the *Neue Zeit.*

When the political struggle of the working class—wrote Marx, ridiculing the Anarchists for their repudiation of political action—assumes a revolutionary form, when the workers set up in place of the dictatorship of the bourgeoisie their revolutionary dictatorship, then they commit the terrible crime of outraging principle, for in order to satisfy their wretched, vulgar, everyday needs, in order to break down the resistance of the bourgeoisie, they give the state a revolutionary and transitional form, instead of laying down arms and abolishing the state. . . .*

It was exclusively against this kind of "abolition" of the state, that Marx fought, refuting the Anarchists! He fought, not against the theory of the disappearance of the state when classes disappear, or of its abolition when classes have been abolished, but against the proposition that the workers should deny themselves the use of arms, the use of organised force, that is, *the use of the state,* for the purpose of "breaking down the resistance of the bourgeoisie."

* *Neue Zeit*, XXXII-1, 1913-1914, p. 40.

In order that the true sense of his fight against the Anarchists might not be perverted, Marx purposely emphasises the "revolutionary and *transitional* form" of the state necessary for the proletariat. The proletariat needs the state only for a while. We do not at all disagree with the Anarchists on the question of the abolition of the state as an *aim*. We maintain that, to achieve this aim, temporary use must be made of the instruments, means, and methods of the state power *against* the exploiters, just as the dictatorship of the oppressed class is temporarily necessary for the annihilation of classes. Marx chooses the sharpest and clearest way of stating his position against the Anarchists: when they have cast off the yoke of the capitalists, ought the workers to "lay down arms," or ought they to use them against the capitalists in order to crush their resistance? But what is the systematic use of arms by one class against the other, if not a "transitional form" of state?

Let every Social-Democrat ask himself: Was *that* the way in which he approached the question of the state in his discussion with the Anarchists? Was *that* the way in which the vast majority of the official Social-Democratic parties of the Second International approached it?

Engels develops these same ideas in even greater detail and more simply. He first of all ridicules the muddled ideas of the Proudhonists, who called themselves "anti-authoritarians," *i.e.*, they denied every kind of authority, every kind of subordination, every kind of power. Take a factory, a railway, a vessel on the high seas, said Engels—is it not clear that not one of these complex technical units, based on the use of machines and the ordered co-operation of many people, could function without a certain amount of subordination and, consequently, without some authority or power?

When I put these arguments—writes Engels—up against the most rabid anti-authoritarians, they are only able to give me the following answer: Ah! that is true, but here it is not a case of authority conferred on the delegates, *but of a commission* which we give them. These people think that they can change a thing by changing its name. . . .

Having thus shown that authority and autonomy are relative terms, that the sphere of their application varies with the various phases of social development, that it is absurd to take them as absolute concepts; having added that the sphere of the application of machinery and large-scale production is ever extending, Engels passes from a general discussion of authority to the question of the state.

If the autonomists—he writes—had been content to say that the social organisation of the future would permit authority only within the limits in which the relations of production made it inevitable, then it would have been possible to come to an understanding with them; but they are blind to all facts which make authority necessary, and they fight passionately against the word.

Why do the anti-authoritarians not confine themselves to crying out against political authority, against the state? All Socialists are agreed that the state, and political authority along with it, will disappear as the result of the coming social revolution, i.e., that public functions will lose their political character and be transformed into simple administrative functions of watching over social interests. But the anti-authoritarians demand that the political state should be abolished at one stroke, even before the social relations which gave birth to it have been abolished. They demand that the first act of the social revolution should be the abolition of authority.

Have these gentlemen ever seen a revolution? Revolution is undoubtedly the most authoritative thing possible. It is an act in which one section of the population imposes its will on the other by means of rifles, bayonets, cannon, i.e., by highly authoritative means, and the victorious party is inevitably forced to maintain its supremacy by means of that fear which its arms inspire in the reactionaries. Would the Paris Commune have lasted a single day had it not relied on the authority of the armed people against the bourgeoisie? Are we not, on the contrary, entitled to blame the Commune for not having made sufficient use of this authority? And so: either—or: either the anti-authoritarians do not know what they are talking about, in which case they merely sow confusion; or they do know, in which case they are betraying the cause of the proletariat. In either case they serve only the interests of reaction.*

In this discussion, questions are touched upon which must be examined in connection with the subject of the interrelation of politics and economics during the "withering away" of the state. (The next chapter is devoted to this subject.) Such are the questions of the transformation of public functions from political into simply administrative ones, and of the "political state." This last term, particularly liable to cause misunderstanding, indicates the process of the withering away of the state: the dying state, at a certain stage of its withering away, can be called a non-political state.

The most remarkable point in our quotation from Engels is again the way he states the case against the Anarchists. Social-Democrats, desiring to be disciples of Engels, have discussed this question with the Anarchists millions of times since 1873, but they have *not* discussed it as Marxists can and should. The Anarchist idea of the abolition of the state is muddled and *non-revolutionary*—that is how Engels put it. It is precisely the revolution, in its rise and development, with its specific tasks in relation to violence, authority, power, the state, that the Anarchists do not wish to see.

The customary criticism of Anarchism by modern Social-Demo-

* *Ibid.*, p. 39.

crats has been reduced to the purest philistine vulgarity: "We recognise the state, whereas the Anarchists do not." Naturally, such vulgarity cannot but repel revolutionary workingmen who think at all. Engels says something different. He emphasises that all Socialists recognise the disappearance of the state as a result of the Socialist revolution. He then deals with the concrete question of the revolution—that very question which, as a rule, the Social-Democrats, because of their opportunism, evade, leaving it, so to speak, exclusively for the Anarchists "to work out." And in thus formulating the question, Engels takes the bull by the horns: ought not the Commune to have made *more* use of the *revolutionary* power of the *state, i.e.,* of the proletariat armed and organised as the ruling class?

Prevailing official Social-Democracy usually dismissed the question as to the concrete tasks of the proletariat in the revolution either with an inane philistine shrug, or, at the best, with the evasive sophism, "Wait and see." And the Anarchists were thus justified in saying about such a Social-Democracy that it had betrayed the task of educating the working class for the revolution. Engels makes use of the experience of the last proletarian revolution for the particular purpose of making a concrete analysis as to what the proletariat should do in relation both to the banks and the state, and how it should do it.

3. LETTER TO BEBEL

One of the most remarkable, if not the most remarkable observation on the state to be found in the works of Marx and Engels is contained in the following passage of Engels' letter to Bebel dated March 18-28, 1875. This letter, we may remark in passing, was first published, so far as we know, by Bebel in the second volume of his memoirs (*Aus meinen Leben*), published in 1911, *i.e.,* thirty-six years after it had been written and mailed.

Engels wrote to Bebel, criticising that same draft of the Gotha Programme which Marx also criticised in his famous letter to Bracke; referring particularly to the question of the state, Engels said:

... The people's free state has been transformed into a free state. According to the grammatical meaning of the words, the free state is one in which the state is free in relation to its citizens, *i.e.,* a state with a despotic government. It would be well to throw overboard all this chatter about the state, especially after the Commune, which was no longer a state in the proper sense of the word. The Anarchists have too long thrown this "people's state" into our teeth, although already in Marx's work against Proudhon, and then in the *Communist Manifesto*, it was stated definitely that, with the introduction of the Socialist order of society, the state will dissolve of itself [*sich auflöst*] and disappear. As the state is only a transitional phenomenon which must be made use of in struggle, in the revolution, in order forcibly to crush our antagonists, it is pure absurdity to speak of a people's free state. As long as the proletariat still *needs* the state, it needs it, not in the interests of freedom, but for the purpose of crushing its antagonists; and as soon as it becomes possible to speak of freedom, then the state, as such, ceases to exist. We would, therefore, suggest that everywhere the word "state" be replaced by "community" [*Gemeinwesen*], a fine old German word, which corresponds to the French word "commune." *

One must bear in mind that this letter refers to the party programme which Marx criticised in his letter dated only a few weeks later than the above (Marx's letter is dated May 5, 1875), and that Engels was living at the time with Marx in London. Consequently, when he says "we" in the last sentence, Engels undoubtedly suggests to the leader of the German workers' party, both in his own and in Marx's name, that the word "state" should be *struck out of the programme* and replaced by "*community.*"

What a howl about "Anarchism" would be raised by the leaders of present-day "Marxism," adulterated to meet the requirements of the opportunists, if such a rectifying of the programme were suggested to them!

Let them howl. The bourgeoisie will praise them for it.

But we shall go on with our work. In revising the programme of our party, the advice of Engels and Marx absolutely must be taken into consideration in order to come nearer to the truth, to re-establish Marxism, to purge it of distortions, to direct more correctly the struggle of the working class for its liberation. Among the Bolsheviks there will certainly be none opposed to the advice of Engels and Marx. Difficulties may, perhaps, crop up only regarding terminology. In German there are two words meaning "community," ** of which Engels used the one which does not denote a single community, but the totality, the system of communities. In Russian there is no such word, and perhaps we may have to decide to use the French word "commune," although this also has its drawbacks.

"The Commune was no longer a state in the proper sense of the word"—this is Engels' most important statement, theoretically speak-

---

* *Aus meinen Leben*, pp. 321-322.
** *Gemeinde* and *Gemeinwesen.—Ed.*

ing. After what has been presented above, this statement is perfectly clear. The Commune _ceased_ to be a state in so far as it had to repress, not the majority of the population but a minority (the exploiters); it had broken the bourgeois state machinery; in the place of a _special_ repressive force, the whole population itself came onto the scene. All this is a departure from the state in its proper sense. And had the Commune asserted itself as a lasting power, remnants of the state would of themselves have "withered away" within it; it would not have been necessary to "abolish" its institutions; they would have ceased to function in proportion as less and less was left for them to do.

"The Anarchists throw this 'people's state' into our teeth." In saying this, Engels has in mind especially Bakunin and his attacks on the German Social-Democrats. Engels admits these attacks to be justified _in so far_ as the "people's state" is as senseless and as much a deviation from Socialism as the "people's free state." Engels tries to improve the struggle of the German Social-Democrats against the Anarchists, to make this struggle correct in principle, to purge it of opportunist prejudices concerning the "state." Alas! Engels' letter has been pigeonholed for thirty-six years. We shall see below that, even after the publication of Engels' letter, Kautsky obstinately repeats in essence the very mistakes against which Engels warned.

Bebel replied to Engels in a letter, dated September 21, 1875, in which, among other things, he wrote that he "fully agreed" with Engels' criticism of the draft programme, and that he had reproached Liebknecht for his readiness to make concessions.* But if we take Bebel's pamphlet, _Unsere Ziele,_ we find there absolutely wrong views regarding the state:

The state must be transformed from one based on _class domination_ into a _people's state._**

This is printed in the _ninth_ (the ninth!) edition of Bebel's pamphlet. Small wonder that such constantly repeated opportunist views regarding the state were absorbed by German Social-Democracy, especially as Engels' revolutionary interpretations were safely pigeonholed, and all the conditions of everyday life were such as to "wean" the people from revolution for a long time!

* _Ibid.,_ Vol. II, p. 334.
** _Unsere Ziele,_ 1886, p. 14.

4. CRITICISM OF THE DRAFT OF THE ERFURT PROGRAMME

In analysing the doctrines of Marxism on the state, the criticism of the draft of the Erfurt Programme sent by Engels to Kautsky on June 29, 1891, a criticism published only ten years later in *Neue Zeit*, cannot be overlooked; for this criticism is mainly concerned with the *opportunist* views of Social-Democracy regarding questions of *state* organisation.[5]

We may note in passing that in the field of economics Engels also makes an exceedingly valuable observation, which shows how attentively and thoughtfully he followed the changes in modern capitalism, and how he was able, in a measure, to foresee the problems of our own, the imperialist, epoch. Here is the point: touching on the word "planlessness" (*Planlosigkeit*) used in the draft programme, as characteristic of capitalism, Engels writes:

When we pass from joint-stock companies to trusts which control and monopolise whole branches of industry, not only private production comes to an end at that point, but also planlessness.*

Here we have what is most essential in the theoretical appreciation of the latest phase of capitalism, *i.e.*, imperialism, *viz.*, that capitalism becomes monopoly *capitalism*. This fact must be emphasised because the bourgeois reformist view that monopoly capitalism or state-monopoly capitalism is *no longer* capitalism, but can already be termed "state Socialism," or something of that sort, is a very widespread error. The trusts, of course, have not created, do not create now, and cannot create full and complete planning. But, however much of a plan they may create, however closely capitalist magnates may estimate in advance the extent of production on a national and even international scale, and however systematically they may regulate it, we still remain *under capitalism*—capitalism, it is true, in its new stage, but still, unquestionably, capitalism. The "proximity" of *such* capitalism to Socialism should serve for the real representatives of the proletariat as an argument proving the nearness, ease, feasibility and urgency of the Socialist revolution, and not at all as an argument for tolerating a repudiation of such a revolution or for making capitalism more attractive, in which work all the reformists are engaged.

---

* *Neue Zeit*, XX-1, 1901-1902, p. 8. [Karl Marx and Friedrich Engels, *Critique of the Social-Democratic Programmes*, London and New York, 1933.—*Ed.*]

But to return to the question of the state. Engels makes here three kinds of valuable suggestions: first, as regards a republic; second, as to the connection between the national question and the form of state; and third, as to local self-government.

As to a republic, Engels made this point the centre of gravity of his criticism of the draft of the Erfurt Programme. And when we remember what importance the Erfurt Programme has acquired in international Social-Democracy, how it has become the model for the whole of the Second International, it may, without exaggeration, be said that Engels thereby criticised the opportunism of the whole Second International.

The political demands of the draft—Engels writes—have one great defect. The point that should particularly have been stated *is not among them* [Engels' italics].*

And, later on, he makes it clear that the German constitution is but a copy of the reactionary constitution of 1850; that the Reichstag is only, as Wilhelm Liebknecht put it, "the fig-leaf of absolutism"; and that to wish "to transform all the means of production into public property" on the basis of a constitution which legalises the existence of petty states and the federation of petty German states, is an "obvious absurdity."

"It is dangerous to touch on this subject," Engels adds, knowing full well that it is impossible, for police reasons, to include in the programme an openly stated demand for a republic in Germany. But Engels does not rest content with this obvious consideration which satisfies "everybody." He continues:

And yet in one way or another the question must be tackled. How necessary this is is shown precisely at this moment by the opportunism which is gaining ground [*einreissend*] in a large section of the Social-Democratic press. Because they fear the re-enactment of the anti-Socialist law, because they have in mind all kinds of premature declarations made when that law was in force, now all at once we are told that the legal situation now existing in Germany can suffice the party for the realisation of all its demands by peaceful methods.

That the German Social-Democrats were actuated by fear of the renewal of the exception law, this fundamental fact Engels stresses particularly, and, without hesitation, he calls this opportunism, declaring that just because of the absence of a republic and freedom in Germany, the dreams of a "peaceful" path were perfectly absurd.

* *Ibid.—Ed.*

Engels is sufficiently careful not to tie his hands. He adm
republican or very free countries "one can conceive" (
ceive"!) of a peaceful development towards Socialism, b
many, he repeats:

> ... In Germany, where the government is almost all-powerful and the
> Reichstag and all other representative bodies have no real power, to proclaim
> such a thing in Germany—and moreover when there is no need to do so—
> is to remove the fig-leaf from absolutism, and to screen its nakedness by one's
> own body.

The great majority of the official leaders of the German Social-
Democratic Party, who pigeonholed this advice, has indeed proved
to be a screen for absolutism.

> Such a policy can only lead their own party permanently astray. General
> and abstract political questions are pushed into the foreground, thus covering
> up the immediate concrete issues, the issues which, at the first great events,
> at the first political crisis, put themselves on the order of the day. What else
> can come of it but that suddenly, at the decisive moment, the party will be
> helpless and that there will be lack of clarity and unity on the most decisive
> points, for the reason that these points have never been discussed. . . .
> This neglect of the great fundamental issues for momentary day-to-day
> interests, this striving and struggling for momentary success without regard
> to further consequences, this sacrifice of the future of the movement for the
> sake of its immediate position may be "honestly" meant, but opportunism it
> is and remains, and "honest" opportunism is perhaps the most dangerous of
> all. . . .
> If anything is certain, it is that our party and the working class can only
> come to power under the form of the democratic republic. This is, indeed,
> the specific form for the dictatorship of the proletariat, as has already been
> shown by the great French Revolution. . . .*

Engels repeats here in a particularly emphatic form the fundamental idea which runs like a red thread throughout all Marx's
work, namely, that the democratic republic is the nearest approach
to the dictatorship of the proletariat. For such a republic—without
in the least setting aside the domination of capital, and, therefore,
the oppression of the masses and the class struggle—inevitably leads
to such an extension, development, unfolding and sharpening of that
struggle that, as soon as the possibility arises for satisfying the
fundamental interests of the oppressed masses, this possibility is
realised inevitably and solely in the dictatorship of the proletariat,
in the guidance of these masses by the proletariat. These also have
been, for the whole of the Second International, "forgotten words"
of Marxism, and this forgetting was demonstrated with particular

*Ibid.—Ed

.vidness by the history of the Menshevik Party during the first half year of the Russian Revolution of 1917.

On the question of a federal republic, in connection with the national composition of the population, Engels wrote:

What should take the place of present-day Germany (with its reactionary monarchical constitution and its equally reactionary division into petty states, which perpetuates all that is specifically Prussian instead of merging it in Germany as a whole)? In my view, the proletariat can use only the form of the one and indivisible republic. In the gigantic territory of the United States a federal republic is still, on the whole, a necessity, although in the Eastern States it is already becoming a hindrance. It would be a step forward in England, where the two islands are peopled by four nations and in spite of a single Parliament three different systems of legislation exist side by side even today. In little Switzerland, it has long been a hindrance, tolerable only because Switzerland is content to be purely a passive member of the European state system. For Germany, federation of the Swiss type would be an enormous step backward. Two points distinguish a federal state from a unitary state: that each separate federated state, each canton, has its own civil and criminal legislation and judicial system, and then, that alongside of a popular chamber there is also a house of representatives from the states, in which each canton, large or small, votes as such. Fortunately, we have got over the first, and we shall not be so childish as to introduce it again; and we have the second in the Federal Council [*Bundesrat*] and could very well do without it, especially as our "federal state" [*Bundestaat*] already forms the transition to the unitary State. And it is not our task to reverse from above the revolution carried out in 1866 and 1870, but to give it its necessary completion and improvements through a movement from below.*

Engels not only shows no indifference to the question of the forms of state, but, on the contrary, tries to analyse with the utmost care the transitional forms, in order to establish in accordance with the concrete historical peculiarities of each separate case, *from what and to what* the given transitional form is evolving.

From the point of view of the proletariat and the proletarian revolution, Engels, like Marx, insists on democratic centralism, on one indivisible republic. The federal republic he considers either as an exception and a hindrance to development, or as a transitional form from a monarchy to a centralised republic, as a "step forward" under certain special conditions. And among these special conditions, the national question arises.

Engels, like Marx, in spite of their ruthless criticism of the reactionary nature of small states, and, in certain concrete cases, the screening of this by the national question, never shows a trace of desire to ignore the national question—a desire of which the Dutch

* *Ibid.—Ed.*

and Polish Marxists are often guilty, as a result of their most ju
fiable opposition to the narrow philistine nationalism of "their" l
states.

Even in England, where geographical conditions, common language, and the history of many centuries would seem to have put
"an end" to the national question in the separate small divisions of
England—even here Engels is cognisant of the patent fact that the
national question has not yet been overcome, and recognises, in consequence, that the establishment of a federal republic would be a
"step forward." Of course, there is no trace here of refusing to
criticise the defects of the federal republic or to conduct the most
determined propaganda and fight for a united and centralised democratic republic.

But Engels by no means understands democratic centralism in the
bureaucratic sense in which this term is used by bourgeois and petty-
bourgeois ideologists, including Anarchists. Centralism does not,
with Engels, in the least exclude such wide local self-government
which combines a voluntary defence of the unity of the state by the
"communes" and districts with the complete abolition of all bureaucracy and all "commanding" from above.

... So, then, a unitary republic—writes Engels, setting forth the program-
matic views of Marxism on the state—but not in the sense of the present
French Republic, which is nothing but the Empire established in 1798 minus
the Emperor. From 1792 to 1798 each Department of France, each local area
[*Gemeinde*] enjoyed complete self-government on the American model, and
this is what we too must have. How self-government is to be organised, and
how we can manage without a bureaucracy, has been demonstrated to us by
America and the first French Republic, and is being demonstrated even today
by Australia, Canada and the other English colonies. And a provincial and
local self-government of this type is far freer than, for example, Swiss federalism, in which it is true the canton is very independent in relation to the *Bund*
(*i.e.*, the federated state as a whole), but is also independent in relation to the
district and the local area. The cantonal governments appoint the district
governors [*Staathalter*] and prefects—a feature which is unknown in English-
speaking countries, and which in the future we shall have to abolish here,
along with the Prussian *Landräte* and *Regierungsräte* [Commissaries, district
police chiefs, governors, and in general all officials appointed from above].*

In accordance with this, Engels suggests the following wording for
the clause in the programme regarding self-government:

Complete self-government for the provinces, districts, and local areas through
officials elected by universal suffrage. The abolition of all local and provincial
authorities appointed by the state.

* *Ibid.—Ed.*

In the *Pravda* (No. 68, June 10, 1917),[*] suppressed by the government of Kerensky and other "Socialist" Ministers, I have already had occasion to point out how in this connection (not by any means in this alone) our sham Socialist representatives of the sham-revolutionary sham-democracy have scandalously departed *from democracy*. Naturally, people who have bound themselves by a "coalition" with the imperialist bourgeoisie remained deaf to this criticism.

It is highly important to note that Engels, armed with facts, disproves by a telling example the superstition, very widespread especially among the petty-bourgeois democracy, that a federal republic necessarily means a greater amount of freedom than a centralised republic. This is not true. It is disproved by the facts cited by Engels regarding the centralised French Republic of 1792-1798 and the federal Swiss Republic. The really democratic centralised republic gave *more* freedom than the federal republic. In other words, the *greatest* amount of local, provincial and other freedom known in history was granted by a *centralised*, and not by a federal republic.

Insufficient attention has been and is being paid to this fact in our party propaganda and agitation, as, indeed, to the whole question of federal and centralised republics and local self-government.

5. The 1891 Preface to Marx's *Civil War in France*

In his preface to the third edition of *The Civil War in France* (this preface is dated March 18, 1891, and was originally published in the *Neue Zeit*), Engels, with many other interesting remarks, made in passing, on questions of the attitude towards the state, gives a remarkably striking résumé of the lessons of the Commune. This résumé, confirmed by all the experience of the period of twenty years separating the author from the Commune, and directed particularly against the "superstitious faith in the state" so widely diffused in Germany, can justly be called the *last word* of Marxism on the question dealt with here.

In France, Engels observes the workers were armed after every revolution,

and therefore the disarming of the workers was the first commandment for whatever bourgeois was at the helm of the state. Hence, after each revolution won by the workers, a new struggle, ending with the defeat of the workers.[6] [**]

[*] See V. I. Lenin, *Collected Works*, Vol. XX, Book II, pp. 148-150.—*Ed.*
[**] *The Civil War in France.*—*Ed.*

This summing up of the experience of bourgeois revolutions is as concise as it is expressive. The essence of the whole matter—also, by the way, of the question of the state (*has the oppressed class arms?*)—is here remarkably well defined. It is just this essential thing which is most ignored both by professors under the influence of bourgeois ideology and by the petty-bourgeois democrats. In the Russian Revolution of 1917, the honour (Cavaignac honour) of babbling out this secret of bourgeois revolutions fell to the Menshevik, "also-Marxist," Tsereteli. In his "historic" speech of June 22, Tsereteli blurted out the decision of the bourgeoisie to disarm the Petrograd workers—referring, of course, to this decision as his own, and as a vital necessity for the "state"! [7]

Tsereteli's historic speech of June 22 will certainly constitute for every historian of the Revolution of 1917 one of the clearest illustrations of how the bloc of Socialist-Revolutionaries and Mensheviks, led by Mr. Tsereteli, went over to the side of the bourgeoisie *against* the revolutionary proletariat.

Another incidental remark of Engels', also connected with the question of the state, deals with religion. It is well known that German Social-Democracy, in proportion as it began to decay and become more and more opportunist, slid down more and more frequently to the philistine misinterpretation of the celebrated formula: "Religion is a private matter." That is, this formula was twisted to mean that *even for the party* of the revolutionary proletariat the question of religion was a private matter! It was against this complete betrayal of the revolutionary programme of the proletariat that Engels revolted. In 1891 he only saw the *very feeble* beginnings of opportunism in his party, and therefore he expressed himself on the subject most cautiously:

As almost without exception workers or recognised representatives of the workers sat in the Commune, its decisions bore a decidedly proletarian character. Either they decreed reforms which the republican bourgeoisie had failed to pass only out of cowardice, but which provided a necessary basis for the free activity of the working class—such as the adoption of the principle that *in relation to the state*, religion is a purely private affair—or they promulgated decrees directly in the interests of the working class and to some extent cutting deeply into the old order of society.*

Engels deliberately emphasised the words "in relation to the state," as a straight thrust at the heart of German opportunism, which had declared religion to be a private matter *in relation to the party*,

* *Ibid.—Ed.*

thus lowering the party of the revolutionary proletariat to the most vulgar "free-thinking" philistine level, ready to allow a non-denominational status, but renouncing all *party* struggle against the religious opium which stupefies the people.

The future historian of German Social-Democracy in investigating the basic causes of its shameful collapse in 1914, will find no little material of interest on this question, beginning with the evasive declarations in the articles of the ideological leader of the party, Kautsky, which opened the door wide to opportunism, and ending with the attitude of the party towards the *Los-von-Kirche Bewegung* (the movement for the disestablishment of the church) in 1913.

But let us see how, twenty years after the Commune, Engels summed up its lessons for the fighting proletariat.

Here are the lessons to which Engels attached prime importance:

... It was precisely this oppressive power of the former centralised government—the army, political police and bureaucracy which Napoleon had created in 1798 and since then had been taken over as a welcome instrument by every new government and used against its opponents—it was precisely this power which should have fallen everywhere, as it had already fallen in Paris.

The Commune was compelled to recognise from the outset that the working class, once come to power, could not carry on business with the old state machine; that, in order not to lose again its own position of power which it had but just conquered, this working class must, on the one hand, set aside all the old repressive machinery previously used against itself, and on the other, safeguard itself against its own deputies and officials by declaring them all, without any exception, subject to recall at any moment. ...

Engels emphasises again and again that not only in a monarchy, but *also in a democratic republic,* the state remains a state, *i.e.,* it retains its fundamental and characteristic feature of transforming the officials, "the servants of society," its organs, into the *masters* of society.

Against this transformation of the state and the organs of the state from servants of society into masters of society—a process which had been inevitable in all previous states—the Commune made use of two infallible remedies. In the first place, it filled all posts—administrative, judicial and educational—by election on the basis of universal suffrage of all concerned, with the right of these electors to recall their delegate at any time. And in the second place, all officials, high or low, were paid only the wages received by other workers. The highest salary paid by the Commune to any one was 6,000 francs.* In

* Nominally this means about 2,400 rubles a year; according to the present rate of exchange about 6,000 rubles. Those Bolsheviks who propose a salary of 9,000 rubles for members of the municipal administration, for instance, instead of suggesting a maximum salary of 6,000 rubles *for the whole of the state*—a sum quite sufficient for anybody, are making quite an unpardonable error.[8]

this way, an effective barrier to place-hunting and careerism was set up, even apart from the imperative mandates to delegates to representative bodies which were also added in profusion. . . .*

Engels approaches here the interesting boundary line where consistent democracy is, on the one hand, *transformed* into Socialism, and on the other, it *demands* the introduction of Socialism. For, in order to destroy the state, it is necessary to convert the functions of public service into such simple operations of control and accounting as are within the reach of the vast majority of the population, and, ultimately, of every single individual. And, in order to do away completely with careerism it must be made *impossible* for an "honourable," though unsalaried, post in the public service to be used as a springboard to a highly profitable post in the banks or the joint-stock companies, as happens *constantly* in all the freest capitalist countries.

But Engels does not make the mistake made, for instance, by some Marxists in dealing with the right of a nation to self-determination: that this is impossible under capitalism and will be unnecessary under Socialism. Such an apparently clever, but really incorrect statement might be repeated of *any* democratic institution, including moderate salaries for officials; for, under capitalism, fully consistent democracy is impossible, while under Socialism all democracy *withers away*.

This is a sophism, comparable to the old humorous problem of whether a man is becoming bald if he loses one hair.

To develop democracy *to its logical conclusion*, to find the *forms* for this development, to test them by practice, and so forth—all this is one of the fundamental tasks of the struggle for the social revolution. Taken separately, no kind of democracy will yield Socialism. But in actual life democracy will never be "taken separately"; it will be "taken together" with other things, it will exert *its* influence on economic life, stimulating its reorganisation; it will be subjected, in its turn, to the influence of economic development, and so on. Such is the dialectics of living history.

Engels continues:

This shattering [*Sprengung*] of the former state power and its replacement by a new and really democratic state is described in detail in the third section of *The Civil War*. But it was necessary here once more to dwell briefly on some of its features, because in Germany particularly the superstitious faith in

* *Ibid.—Ed.*

the state has been carried over from philosophy into the general consciousness of the bourgeoisie and even of many workers. According to the philosophical conception, the state is the "realisation of the idea" or, translated into philosophical language, the Kingdom of God on earth; the sphere in which eternal truth and justice is, or should be, realised. And from this then follows a superstitious reverence for the state and for everything connected with it, which takes root the more readily as people from their childhood are accustomed to imagine that the affairs and interests common to the whole of society could not be managed and safeguarded in any other way than as in the past, that is, through the state and its well-paid officials. And people think they are taking quite an extraordinarily bold step forward when they rid themselves of faith in a hereditary monarchy and become partisans of a democratic republic. In reality, however, the state is nothing more than a machine for the oppression of one class by another, and indeed in the democratic republic no less than in the monarchy; and at best an evil, inherited by the proletariat after its victorious struggle for class supremacy, whose worst sides the proletariat, just like the Commune, will have at the earliest possible moment to lop off, until such time as a new generation, reared under new and free social conditions, will be able to throw on the scrap-heap all this state rubbish.*

Engels cautioned the Germans, in the event of the monarchy being replaced by a republic, not to forget the fundamentals of Socialism on the question of the state in general. His warnings now read like a direct lecture to Messrs. Tsereteli and Chernov, who revealed in their coalition tactics a superstitious faith in, and a respect for, the state!

Two more points. First: when Engels says that in a democratic republic, "no less" than in a monarchy, the state remains a "machine for the oppression of one class by another," this by no means signifies that the *form* of oppression is a matter of indifference to the proletariat, as some Anarchists "teach." A wider, freer and more open *form* of the class struggle and of class oppression enormously assists the proletariat in its struggle for the abolition of all classes.

Second: why only a new generation will be able completely to throw out all the state rubbish—this question is bound up with the question of overcoming democracy, to which we now turn.

6. Engels on the Overcoming of Democracy

Engels had occasion to speak on this subject in connection with the question of the *scientific* incorrectness of the term "Social-Democrat."

In the introduction to an edition of his articles of the 'seventies on

* *Ibid.—Ed.*

various subjects, mainly on international questions (*Internationales aus dem Volkstaat*), dated January 3, 1894, *i.e.*, written a year and a half before his death, Engels wrote that in all his articles he used the word "Communist," *not* "Social-Democrat," because at that time it was the Proudhonists in France and the Lassalleans in Germany who called themselves Social-Democrats.

> . . . For Marx and me—Engels writes—it was therefore quite impossible to choose such an elastic term to characterise our special point of view. Today things are different, and the word ("Social-Democrat") may perhaps pass muster [*mag passieren*], however unsuitable [*unpassend*] it still is for a party whose economic programme is not merely Socialist in general, but directly Communist, and whose ultimate political aim is to overcome the whole state, and therefore democracy as well. The names of *real* [Engels' italics] political parties, however, are never wholly appropriate; the party develops. while the name persists.

The dialectician Engels remains true to dialectics to the end of his days. Marx and I, he says, had a splendid, scientifically exact name for the party, but there was no real party, *i.e.*, no proletarian mass party. Now, at the end of the nineteenth century, there is a real party, but its name is scientifically inexact. Never mind, "it will pass muster," only let the party *grow*, do not let the scientific inexactness of its name be hidden from it, and do not let it hinder its development in the right direction!

Perhaps, indeed, some humourist might comfort us Bolsheviks in the manner of Engels: we have a real party, it is developing splendidly; even such a meaningless and awkward term as "Bolshevik" will "pass muster," although it expresses nothing but the purely accidental fact that at the Brussels-London Congress of 1903 we had a majority. . . .* Perhaps now, when the July and August persecutions of our party by republican and "revolutionary" petty-bourgeois democracy have made the word "Bolshevik" such a universally respected name; when, in addition, these persecutions have signalised such a great historical step forward made by our party in its *actual* development, perhaps now even I would hesitate to repeat my April suggestion as to changing the name of our party. Perhaps I would propose a "compromise" to our comrades, to call ourselves the Communist Party, but to retain the word "Bolsheviks" in brackets. . . .

---

* Lenin and his followers among the delegates at this congress secured a majority on a fundamental organisational political question and were afterwards called *Bolsheviks*, from the Russian word *Bolshinstvo*, meaning majority; the adherents of the opposite group were called Mensheviks, from the Russian word *Menshinstvo*, meaning minority.—*Ed.*

But the question of the name of the party is incomparably less important than the question of the relation of the revolutionary proletariat to the state.

In the current arguments about the state, the mistake is constantly made against which Engels cautions here, and which we have indicated above, namely, it is constantly forgotten that the destruction of the state means also the destruction of democracy; that the withering away of the state also means the withering away of democracy.

At first sight such a statement seems exceedingly strange and incomprehensible; indeed, some one may even begin to fear lest we be expecting the advent of such an order of society in which the principle of the subordination of the minority to the majority will not be respected—for is not a democracy just the recognition of this principle?

No, democracy is *not* identical with the subordination of the minority to the majority. Democracy is a *state* recognising the subordination of the minority to the majority, *i.e.*, an organisation for the systematic use of *violence* by one class against the other, by one part of the population against another.

We set ourselves the ultimate aim of destroying the state, *i.e.*, every organised and systematic violence, every use of violence against man in general. We do not expect the advent of an order of society in which the principle of subordination of minority to majority will not be observed. But, striving for Socialism, we are convinced that it will develop into Communism; that, side by side with this, there will vanish all need for force, for the *subjection* of one man to another, and of one part of the population to another, since people will *grow accustomed* to observing the elementary conditions of social existence *without force and without subjection.*

In order to emphasise this element of habit, Engels speaks of a *new generation,* "reared under new and free social conditions," which "will be able to throw on the scrap heap all this state rubbish"— every kind of state, including even the democratic-republican state.

For the elucidation of this, the question of the economic basis of the withering away of the state must be analysed.

CHAPTER V

THE ECONOMIC BASE OF THE WITHERING AWAY OF THE STATE

A MOST detailed elucidation of this question is given by Marx in his *Critique of the Gotha Programme* (letter to Bracke, May 15, 1875, printed only in 1891 in the *Neue Zeit*, IX-1, and in a special Russian edition *). The polemical part of this remarkable work, consisting of a criticism of Lassalleanism, has, so to speak, overshadowed its positive part, namely, the analysis of the connection between the development of Communism and the withering away of the state.

1. FORMULATION OF THE QUESTION BY MARX

From a superficial comparison of the letter of Marx to Bracke (May 15, 1875) with Engels' letter to Bebel (March 28, 1875), analysed above, it might appear that Marx was much more "pro-state" than Engels, and that the difference of opinion between the two writers on the question of the state is very considerable.

Engels suggests to Bebel that all the chatter about the state should be thrown overboard; that the word "state" should be eliminated from the programme and replaced by "community"; Engels even declares that the Commune was really no longer a state in the proper sense of the word. And Marx even speaks of the "future state in Communist society," *i.e.*, he is apparently recognising the necessity of a state even under Communism.

But such a view would be fundamentally incorrect. A closer examination shows that Marx's and Engels' views on the state and its withering away were completely identical, and that Marx's expression quoted above refers merely to this withering away of the state.

It is clear that there can be no question of defining the exact moment of the *future* withering away—the more so as it must obviously be a rather lengthy process. The apparent difference between Marx and Engels is due to the different subjects they dealt with, the different aims they were pursuing. Engels set out to show to Bebel,

* English translation in *Critique of the Social-Democratic Programmes.—Ed.*

in a plain, bold and broad outline, all the absurdity of the current superstitions concerning the state, shared to no small degree by Lassalle himself. Marx, on the other hand, only touches upon *this* question in passing, being interested mainly in another subject—the *evolution* of Communist society.

The whole theory of Marx is an application of the theory of evolution—in its most consistent, complete, well considered and fruitful form—to modern capitalism. It was natural for Marx to raise the question of applying this theory both to the *coming* collapse of capitalism and to the *future* evolution of *future* Communism.

On the basis of what *data* can the future evolution of future Communism be considered?

On the basis of the fact that *it has its origin* in capitalism, that it develops historically from capitalism, that it is the result of the action of a social force to which capitalism *has given birth*. There is no shadow of an attempt on Marx's part to conjure up a Utopia, to make idle guesses about that which cannot be known. Marx treats the question of Communism in the same way as a naturalist would treat the question of the evolution of, say, a new biological species, if he knew that such and such was its origin, and such and such the direction in which it changed.

Marx, first of all, brushes aside the confusion the Gotha Programme brings into the question of the interrelation between state and society.

"Contemporary society" is the capitalist society—he writes—which exists in all civilised countries, more or less free of mediaeval admixture, more or less modified by each country's particular historical development. more or less developed. In contrast with this, the "contemporary state" varies with every state boundary. It is different in the Prusso-German Empire from what it is in Switzerland, and different in England from what it is in the United States. The "contemporary state" is therefore a fiction.

Nevertheless, in spite of the motley variety of their forms, the different states of the various civilised countries all have this in common: they are all based on modern bourgeois society, only a little more or less capitalistically developed. Consequently, they also have certain essential characteristics in common. In this sense, it is possible to speak of the "contemporary state" in contrast to the future, when its present root, bourgeois society, will have perished.

Then the question arises: what transformation will the state undergo in a Communist society? In other words, what social functions analogous to the present functions of the state will then still survive? This question can only be answered scientifically, and however many thousand times the word people is combined with the word state, we get not a flea-jump closer to the problem. . . .*

* *Critique of the Social-Democratic Programmes.—Ed.*

70

Having thus ridiculed all talk about a "people's state," Marx formulates the question and warns us, as it were, that to arrive at a scientific answer one must rely only on firmly established scientific data.

The first fact that has been established with complete exactness by the whole theory of evolution, by science as a whole—a fact which the Utopians forgot, and which is forgotten by the present-day opportunists who are afraid of the Socialist revolution—is that, historically, there must undoubtedly be a special stage or epoch of *transition* from capitalism to Communism.

2. Transition from Capitalism to Communism

Between capitalist and Communist society—Marx continues—lies the period of the revolutionary transformation of the former into the latter. To this also corresponds a political transition period, in which the state can be no other than *the revolutionary dictatorship of the proletariat.**

This conclusion Marx bases on an analysis of the rôle played by the proletariat in modern capitalist society, on the data concerning the evolution of this society, and on the irreconcilability of the opposing interests of the proletariat and the bourgeoisie.

Earlier the question was put thus: to attain its emancipation, the proletariat must overthrow the bourgeoisie, conquer political power and establish its own revolutionary dictatorship.

Now the question is put somewhat differently: the transition from capitalist society, developing towards Communism, towards a Communist society, is impossible without a "political transition period," and the state in this period can only be the revolutionary dictatorship of the proletariat.

What, then, is the relation of this dictatorship to democracy?

We have seen that the *Communist Manifesto* simply places side by side the two ideas: the "transformation of the proletariat into the ruling class" and the "establishment of democracy." On the basis of all that has been said above, one can define more exactly how democracy changes in the transition from capitalism to Communism.

In capitalist society, under the conditions most favourable to its development, we have more or less complete democracy in the democratic republic. But this democracy is always bound by the narrow framework of capitalist exploitation, and consequently always re-

* *Ibid.—Ed.*

mains, in reality, a democracy for the minority, only for the possessing classes, only for the rich. Freedom in capitalist society always remains just about the same as it was in the ancient Greek republics: freedom for the slave-owners. The modern wage-slaves, owing to the conditions of capitalist exploitation, are so much crushed by want and poverty that "democracy is nothing to them," "politics is nothing to them"; that, in the ordinary peaceful course of events, the majority of the population is debarred from participating in social and political life.

The correctness of this statement is perhaps most clearly proved by Germany, just because in this state constitutional legality lasted and remained stable for a remarkably long time—for nearly half a century (1871-1914)—and because Social-Democracy in Germany during that time was able to achieve far more than in other countries in "utilising legality," and was able to organise into a political party a larger proportion of the working class than anywhere else in the world.

What, then, is this largest proportion of politically conscious and active wage-slaves that has so far been observed in capitalist society? One million members of the Social-Democratic Party—out of fifteen million wage-workers! Three million organised in trade unions—out of fifteen million!

Democracy for an insignificant minority, democracy for the rich—that is the democracy of capitalist society. If we look more closely into the mechanism of capitalist democracy, everywhere, both in the "petty"—so-called petty—details of the suffrage (residential qualification, exclusion of women, etc.), and in the technique of the representative institutions, in the actual obstacles to the right of assembly (public buildings are not for "beggars"!), in the purely capitalist organisation of the daily press, etc., etc.—on all sides we see restriction after restriction upon democracy. These restrictions, exceptions, exclusions, obstacles for the poor, seem slight, especially in the eyes of one who has himself never known want and has never been in close contact with the oppressed classes in their mass life (and nine-tenths, if not ninety-nine hundredths, of the bourgeois publicists and politicians are of this class), but in their sum total these restrictions exclude and squeeze out the poor from politics and from an active share in democracy.

Marx splendidly grasped this *essence* of capitalist democracy, when, in analysing the experience of the Commune, he said that the oppressed were allowed, once every few years, to decide which particular representatives of the oppressing class should be in parliament to represent and repress them!

But from this capitalist democracy—inevitably narrow, subtly rejecting the poor, and therefore hypocritical and false to the core—progress does not march onward, simply, smoothly and directly, to "greater and greater democracy," as the liberal professors and petty-bourgeois opportunists would have us believe. No, progress marches onward, *i.e.*, towards Communism, through the dictatorship of the proletariat; it cannot do otherwise, for there is no one else and no other way to *break the resistance* of the capitalist exploiters.

But the dictatorship of the proletariat—*i.e.*, the organisation of the vanguard of the oppressed as the ruling class for the purpose of crushing the oppressors—cannot produce merely an expansion of democracy. *Together* with an immense expansion of democracy which *for the first time* becomes democracy for the poor, democracy for the people, and not democracy for the rich folk, the dictatorship of the proletariat produces a series of restrictions of liberty in the case of the oppressors, the exploiters, the capitalists. We must crush them in order to free humanity from wage-slavery; their resistance must be broken by force; it is clear that where there is suppression there is also violence, there is no liberty, no democracy.

Engels expressed this splendidly in his letter to Bebel when he said, as the reader will remember, that "as long as the proletariat still *needs* the state, it needs it not in the interests of freedom, but for the purpose of crushing its antagonists; and as soon as it becomes possible to speak of freedom, then the state, as such, ceases to exist."

Democracy for the vast majority of the people, and suppression by force, *i.e.*, exclusion from democracy, of the exploiters and oppressors of the people—this is the modification of democracy during the *transition* from capitalism to Communism.

Only in Communist society, when the resistance of the capitalists has been completely broken, when the capitalists have disappeared, when there are no classes (*i.e.*, there is no difference between the members of society in their relation to the social means of production), *only then* "the state ceases to exist," and "*it becomes possible to speak of freedom.*" Only then a really full democracy, a democracy without any exceptions, will be possible and will be realised. And only then will democracy itself begin to *wither away* due to the simple fact that, freed from capitalist slavery, from the untold horrors, savagery, absurdities and infamies of capitalist exploitation, people will gradually *become accustomed* to the observance of the elementary rules of social life that have been known for centuries and repeated for thousands of years in all school books; they will become accustomed to observing them without force, without compulsion, without subordination, without the *special apparatus* for compulsion which is called the state.

The expression "the state *withers away*," is very well chosen, for it indicates both the gradual and the elemental nature of the process. Only habit can, and undoubtedly will, have such an effect; for we see around us millions of times how readily people get accustomed to observe the necessary rules of life in common, if there is no exploitation, if there is nothing that causes indignation, that calls forth protest and revolt and has to be *suppressed*.

Thus, in capitalist society we have a democracy that is curtailed, poor, false; a democracy only for the rich, for the minority. The dictatorship of the proletariat, the period of transition to Communism, will, for the first time, produce democracy for the people, for the majority, side by side with the necessary suppression of the minority—the exploiters. Communism alone is capable of giving a really complete democracy, and the more complete it is the more quickly will it become unnecessary and wither away of itself.

In other words: under capitalism we have a state in the proper sense of the word, that is, special machinery for the suppression of one class by another, and of the majority by the minority at that. Naturally, for the successful discharge of such a task as the systematic suppression by the exploiting minority of the exploited majority, the greatest ferocity and savagery of suppression are required, seas of blood are required, through which mankind is marching in slavery, serfdom, and wage-labour.

Again, during the *transition* from capitalism to Communism, suppression is *still* necessary; but it is the suppression of the minority of exploiters by the majority of exploited. A special apparatus, special machinery for suppression, the "state," is *still* necessary, but this is now a transitional state, no longer a state in the usual sense, for the suppression of the minority of exploiters, by the majority of the wage slaves *of yesterday*, is a matter comparatively so easy, simple and natural that it will cost far less bloodshed than the suppression of the risings of slaves, serfs or wage labourers, and will cost mankind far less. This is compatible with the diffusion of democracy among such an overwhelming majority of the population, that the need for *special machinery* of suppression will begin to disappear. The exploiters are, naturally, unable to suppress the people without a most complex machinery for performing this task; but *the people* can suppress the exploiters even with very simple "machinery," almost without any "machinery," without any special apparatus, by the simple *organisation of the armed masses* (such as the Soviets of Workers' and Soldiers' Deputies, we may remark, anticipating a little).

Finally, only Communism renders the state absolutely unnecessary, for there is *no one* to be suppressed—"no one" in the sense of a *class,* in the sense of a systematic struggle with a definite section of the population. We are not Utopians, and we do not in the least deny the possibility and inevitability of excesses on the part of *individual persons,* nor the need to suppress *such* excesses. But, in the first place, no special machinery, no special apparatus of repression is needed for this; this will be done by the armed people itself, as simply and as readily as any crowd of civilised people, even in modern society, parts a pair of combatants or does not allow a woman to be outraged. And, secondly, we know that the fundamental social cause of excesses which consist in violating the rules of social life is the exploitation of the masses, their want and their poverty. With the removal of this chief cause, excesses will inevitably begin to *"wither away."* We do not know how quickly and in what succession, but we know that they will wither away. With their withering away, the state will also *wither away.*

Without going into Utopias, Marx defined more fully what can *now* be defined regarding this future, namely, the difference between the lower and higher phases (degrees, stages) of Communist society.

3. First Phase of Communist Society

In the *Critique of the Gotha Programme,* Marx goes into some detail to disprove the Lassallean idea of the workers' receiving under Socialism the "undiminished" or "full product of their labour." Marx shows that out of the whole of the social labour of society, it is necessary to deduct a reserve fund, a fund for the expansion of production, for the replacement of worn-out machinery, and so on; then, also, out of the means of consumption must be deducted a fund for the expenses of management, for schools, hospitals, homes for the aged, and so on.

Instead of the hazy, obscure, general phrase of Lassalle's—"the full product of his labour for the worker"—Marx gives a sober estimate of exactly how a Socialist society will have to manage its affairs. Marx undertakes a *concrete* analysis of the conditions of life of a society in which there is no capitalism, and says:

> What we are dealing with here [analysing the programme of the party] is not a Communist society which has *developed* on its own foundations, but, on the contrary, one which is just *emerging* from capitalist society, and which therefore in all respects—economic, moral and intellectual—still bears the birthmarks of the old society from whose womb it sprung.*

And it is this Communist society—a society which has just come into the world out of the womb of capitalism, and which, in all respects, bears the stamp of the old society—that Marx terms the "first," or lower, phase of Communist society.

The means of production are no longer the private property of individuals. The means of production belong to the whole of society. Every member of society, performing a certain part of socially-necessary work, receives a certificate from society to the effect that he has done such and such a quantity of work. According to this certificate, he receives from the public warehouses, where articles of consumption are stored, a corresponding quantity of products. Deducting that proportion of labour which goes to the public fund, every worker, therefore, receives from society as much as he has given it.

"Equality" seems to reign supreme.

But when Lassalle, having in view such a social order (generally called Socialism, but termed by Marx the first phase of Communism), speaks of this as "just distribution," and says that this is "the equal right of each to an equal product of labour," Lassalle is mistaken, and Marx exposes his error.

"Equal right," says Marx, we indeed have here; but it is *still* a "bourgeois right," which, like every right, *presupposes inequality*. Every right is an application of the *same* measure to *different* people who, in fact, are not the same and are not equal to one another; this is why "equal right" is really a violation of equality, and an injustice. In effect, every man having done as much social labour

* *Ibid.—Ed.*

as every other, receives an equal share of the social products (with the above-mentioned deductions).

But different people are not alike: one is strong, another is weak; one is married, the other is not; one has more children, another has less, and so on.

> . . . With equal labour—Marx concludes—and therefore an equal share in the social consumption fund, one man in fact receives more than the other, one is richer than the other, and so forth. In order to avoid all these defects, rights, instead of being equal, must be unequal.*

The first phase of Communism, therefore, still cannot produce justice and equality; differences, and unjust differences, in wealth will still exist, but the *exploitation* of man by man will have become impossible, because it will be impossible to seize as private property the *means of production,* the factories, machines, land, and so on. In tearing down Lassalle's petty-bourgeois, confused phrase about "equality" and "justice" *in general,* Marx shows the *course of development* of Communist society, which is forced at first to destroy *only* the "injustice" that consists in the means of production having been seized by private individuals, and which *is not capable* of destroying at once the further injustice consisting in the distribution of the articles of consumption "according to work performed" (and not according to need).

The vulgar economists, including the bourgeois professors and also "our" Tugan-Baranovsky, constantly reproach the Socialists with forgetting the inequality of people and with "dreaming" of destroying this inequality. Such a reproach, as we see, only proves the extreme ignorance of the gentlemen propounding bourgeois ideology.

Marx not only takes into account with the greatest accuracy the inevitable inequality of men; he also takes into account the fact that the mere conversion of the means of production into the common property of the whole of society ("Socialism" in the generally accepted sense of the word) *does not remove* the defects of distribution and the inequality of "bourgeois right" which *continue to rule* as long as the products are divided "according to work performed."

> But these defects—Marx continues—are unavoidable in the first phase of Communist society, when, after long travail, it first emerges from capitalist society. Justice can never rise superior to the economic conditions of society and the cultural development conditioned by them.**

* *Ibid.—Ed.*   ** *Ibid.—Ed.*

And so, in the first phase of Communist society (generally called Socialism) "bourgeois right" is *not* abolished in its entirety, but only in part, only in proportion to the economic transformation so far attained, *i.e.*, only in respect of the means of production. "Bourgeois right" recognises them as the private property of separate individuals. Socialism converts them into common property. *To that extent*, and to that extent alone, does "bourgeois right" disappear.

However, it continues to exist as far as its other part is concerned; it remains in the capacity of regulator (determining factor) distributing the products and allotting labour among the members of society. "He who does not work, shall not eat"—this Socialist principle is *already* realised; "for an equal quantity of labour, an equal quantity of products"—this Socialist principle is also *already* realised. However, this is not yet Communism, and this does not abolish "bourgeois right," which gives to unequal individuals, in return for an unequal (in reality unequal) amount of work, an equal quantity of products.

This is a "defect," says Marx, but it is unavoidable during the first phase of Communism; for, if we are not to fall into Utopianism, we cannot imagine that, having overthrown capitalism, people will at once learn to work for society *without any standards of right;* indeed, the abolition of capitalism *does not immediately lay* the economic foundations for *such* a change.

And there is no other standard yet than that of "bourgeois right." To this extent, therefore, a form of state is still necessary, which, while maintaining public ownership of the means of production, would preserve the equality of labour and equality in the distribution of products.

The state is withering away in so far as there are no longer any capitalists, any classes, and, consequently, no *class* can be suppressed.

But the state has not yet altogether withered away, since there still remains the protection of "bourgeois right" which sanctifies actual inequality. For the complete extinction of the state, complete Communism is necessary.

4. Higher Phase of Communist Society

Marx continues:

In a higher phase of Communist society, when the enslaving subordination of individuals in the division of labour has disappeared, and with it also the antagonism between mental and physical labour; when labour has only a means of living, but itself the first necessity of life; when the all-round development of individuals, the productive forces too and all the springs of social wealth are flowing more freely—it is stage that it will be possible to pass completely beyond the nar of bourgeois rights, and for society to inscribe on its banners. according to his ability; to each according to his needs! *

Only now can we appreciate the full correctness of Engels' remarks in which he mercilessly ridiculed all the absurdity of combining the words "freedom" and "state." While the state exists there is no freedom. When there is freedom, there will be no state.

The economic basis for the complete withering away of the state is that high stage of development of Communism when the antagonism between mental and physical labour disappears, that is to say, when one of the principal sources of modern *social* inequality disappears—a source, moreover, which it is impossible to remove immediately by the mere conversion of the means of production into public property, by the mere expropriation of the capitalists.

This expropriation will make a gigantic development of the productive forces *possible*. And seeing how incredibly, even now, capitalism *retards* this development, how much progress could be made even on the basis of modern technique at the level it has reached, we have a right to say, with the fullest confidence, that the expropriation of the capitalists will inevitably result in a gigantic development of the productive forces of human society. But how rapidly this development will go forward, how soon it will reach the point of breaking away from the division of labour, of removing the antagonism between mental and physical labour, of transforming work into the "first necessity of life"—this we do not and *cannot* know.

Consequently, we have a right to speak solely of the inevitable withering away of the state, emphasising the protracted nature of this process and its dependence upon the rapidity of development of the *higher phase* of Communism; leaving quite open the question of lengths of time, or the concrete forms of withering away, since material for the solution of such questions is *not available.*

The state will be able to wither away completely when society has realised the rule: "From each according to his ability; to each according to his needs," *i.e.*, when people have become accustomed to observe the fundamental rules of social life, and their labour is

* *Ibid.—Ed.*

, productive, that they voluntarily work *according to their ability*. "The narrow horizon of bourgeois rights," which compels one to calculate, with the hard-heartedness of a Shylock, whether he has not worked half an hour more than another, whether he is not getting less pay than another—this narrow horizon will then be left behind. There will then be no need for any exact calculation by society of the quantity of products to be distributed to each of its members; each will take freely "according to his needs."

From the bourgeois point of view, it is easy to declare such a social order "a pure Utopia," and to sneer at the Socialists for promising each the right to receive from society, without any control of the labour of the individual citizen, any quantity of truffles, automobiles, pianos, etc. Even now, most bourgeois "savants" deliver themselves of such sneers, thereby displaying at once their ignorance and their self-seeking defence of capitalism.

Ignorance—for it has never entered the head of any Socialist to "promise" that the highest phase of Communism will arrive; while the great Socialists, in *foreseeing* its arrival, presupposed both a productivity of labour unlike the present and a person not like the present man in the street, capable of spoiling, without reflection, like the seminary students in Pomyalovsky's book,* the stores of social wealth, and of demanding the impossible.

Until the "higher" phase of Communism arrives, the Socialists demand the *strictest* control, *by society and by the state,* of the quantity of labour and the quantity of consumption; only this control must *start* with the expropriation of the capitalists, with the control of the workers over the capitalists, and must be carried out, not by a state of bureaucrats, but by a state of *armed workers.*

Self-seeking defence of capitalism by the bourgeois ideologists (and their hangers-on like Tsereteli, Chernov and Co.) consists in that they *substitute* disputes and discussions about the distant future for the essential imperative questions of present-day policy: the expropriation of the capitalists, the conversion of *all* citizens into workers and employees of *one* huge "syndicate"—the whole state— and the complete subordination of the whole of the work of this syndicate to the really democratic state of the *Soviets of Workers' and Soldiers' Deputies.*

In reality, when a learned professor, and following him some

---

* Pomyalovsky's *Seminary Sketches* depicted a group of student-ruffians who engaged in destroying things for the pleasure it gave them.—*Ed.*

philistine, and following the latter Messrs. Tsereteli and Chernov, talk of the unreasonable Utopias, of the demagogic promises of the Bolsheviks, of the impossibility of "introducing" Socialism, it is the higher stage or phase of Communism which they have in mind, and which no one has ever promised, or even thought of "introducing," for the reason that, generally speaking, it cannot be "introduced."

And here we come to that question of the scientific difference between Socialism and Communism, upon which Engels touched in his above-quoted discussion on the incorrectness of the name "Social-Democrat." The political difference between the first, or lower, and the higher phase of Communism will in time, no doubt, be tremendous; but it would be ridiculous to emphasise it now, under capitalism, and only, perhaps, some isolated Anarchist could invest it with primary importance (if there are still some people among the Anarchists who have learned nothing from the Plekhanov-like conversion of the Kropotkins, the Graveses, the Cornelissens, and other "leading lights" of Anarchism to social-chauvinism or Anarcho-*Jusquaubout*-ism,* as Ge, one of the few Anarchists still preserving honour and conscience, has expressed it).

But the scientific difference between Socialism and Communism is clear. What is generally called Socialism was termed by Marx the "first" or lower phase of Communist society. In so far as the means of production become *public* property, the word "Communism" is also applicable here, providing we do not forget that it is *not* full Communism. The great significance of Marx's elucidations consists in this: that here, too, he consistently applies materialist dialectics, the doctrine of evolution, looking upon Communism as something which evolves *out of* capitalism. Instead of artificial, "elaborate," scholastic definitions and profitless disquisitions on the meaning of words (what Socialism is, what Communism is), Marx gives an analysis of what may be called stages in the economic ripeness of Communism.

In its first phase or first stage Communism *cannot* as yet be economically ripe and entirely free of all tradition and of all taint of capitalism. Hence the interesting phenomenon of Communism retaining, in its first phase, "the narrow horizon of bourgeois rights." Bourgeois rights, with respect to distribution of articles of *consump-*

---

* *Jusquaubout*—combination of the French words meaning "until the end." Anarcho-*Jusquaubout*-ism—Anarcho-until-the-End-ism.—*Ed.*

tion, inevitably presupposes, of course, the existence of the *bourgeois state*, for rights are nothing without an apparatus capable of *enforcing* the observance of the rights.

Consequently, for a certain time not only bourgeois rights, but even the bourgeois state remains under Communism, without the bourgeoisie!

This may look like a paradox, or simply a dialectical puzzle for which Marxism is often blamed by people who would not make the least effort to study its extraordinarily profound content.

But, as a matter of fact, the old surviving in the new confronts us in life at every step, in nature as well as in society. Marx did not smuggle a scrap of "bourgeois" rights into Communism of his own accord; he indicated what is economically and politically inevitable in a society issuing *from the womb* of capitalism.

Democracy is of great importance for the working class in its struggle for freedom against the capitalists. But democracy is by no means a limit one may not overstep; it is only one of the stages in the course of development from feudalism to capitalism, and from capitalism to Communism.

Democracy means equality. The great significance of the struggle of the proletariat for equality, and the significance of equality as a slogan, are apparent, if we correctly interpret it as meaning the abolition of *classes*. But democracy means only *formal* equality. Immediately after the attainment of equality for all members of society *in respect of* the ownership of the means of production, that is, of equality of labour and equality of wages, there will inevitably arise before humanity the question of going further from formal equality to real equality, *i.e.*, to realising the rule, "From each according to his ability; to each according to his needs." By what stages, by means of what practical measures humanity will proceed to this higher aim—this we do not and cannot know. But it is important to realise how infinitely mendacious is the usual bourgeois presentation of Socialism as something lifeless, petrified, fixed once for all, whereas in reality, it is *only* with Socialism that there will commence a rapid, genuine, real mass advance, in which first the *majority* and then the whole of the population will take part—an advance in all domains of social and individual life.

Democracy is a form of the state—one of its varieties. Consequently, like every state, it consists in organised, systematic application of force against human beings. This on the one hand. On the other hand, however, it signifies the formal recognition of the equality of all citizens, the equal right of all to determine the structure and administration of the state. This, in turn, is connected with the fact that, at a certain stage in the development of democracy, it first rallies the proletariat as a revolutionary class against capitalism, and gives it an opportunity to crush, to smash to bits, to wipe off the face of the earth the bourgeois state machinery—even its republican variety: the standing army, the police, and bureaucracy; then it substitutes for all this a *more* democratic, but still a state machinery in the shape of armed masses of workers, which becomes transformed into universal participation of the people in the militia.

Here "quantity turns into quality": *such* a degree of democracy is bound up with the abandonment of the framework of bourgeois society, and the beginning of its Socialist reconstruction. If *every one* really takes part in the administration of the state, capitalism cannot retain its hold. In its turn, capitalism, as it develops, itself creates *prerequisites* for "every one" *to be able* really to take part in the administration of the state. Among such prerequisites are: universal literacy, already realised in most of the advanced capitalist countries, then the "training and disciplining" of millions of workers by the huge, complex, and socialised apparatus of the post-office, the railways, the big factories, large-scale commerce, banking, etc., etc.

With such *economic* prerequisites it is perfectly possible, immediately, within twenty-four hours after the overthrow of the capitalists and bureaucrats, to replace them, in the control of production and distribution, in the business of *control* of labour and products, by the armed workers, by the whole people in arms. (The question of control and accounting must not be confused with the question of the scientifically educated staff of engineers, agronomists and so on. These gentlemen work today, obeying the capitalists; they will work even better tomorrow, obeying the armed workers.)

Accounting and control—these are the *chief* things necessary for the organising and correct functioning of the *first phase* of Communist society. *All* citizens are here transformed into hired employees of the state, which is made up of the armed workers. *All* citizens become employees and workers of *one* national state "syndicate." All that is required is that they should work equally, should regularly do their share of work, and should receive equal pay. The accounting and control necessary for this have been *simplified* by capitalism to the utmost, till they have become the extraordinarily simple operations of watching, recording and issuing receipts, within the reach of anybody who can read and write and knows the first four rules of arithmetic.*

When the *majority* of the people begin everywhere to keep such accounts and maintain such control over the capitalists (now converted into employees) and over the intellectual gentry, who still retain capitalist habits, this control will really become universal, general, national; and there will be no way of getting away from it, there will be "nowhere to go."

The whole of society will have become one office and one factory, with equal work and equal pay.

But this "factory" discipline, which the proletariat will extend to the whole of society after the defeat of the capitalists and the overthrow of the exploiters, is by no means our ideal, or our final aim. It is but a *foothold* necessary for the radical cleansing of society of all the hideousness and foulness of capitalist exploitation, *in order to advance further.*

From the moment when all members of society, or even only the overwhelming majority, have learned how to govern the state *themselves,* have taken this business into their own hands, have "established" control over the insignificant minority of capitalists, over the gentry with capitalist leanings, and the workers thoroughly demoralised by capitalism—from this moment the need for any government begins to disappear. The more complete the democracy, the nearer the moment when it begins to be unnecessary. The more democratic the "state" consisting of armed workers, which is "no longer a state in the proper sense of the word," the more rapidly does *every* state begin to wither away.

For when *all* have learned to manage, and independently are actually managing by themselves social production, keeping accounts, controlling the idlers, the gentlefolk, the swindlers and similar "guardians of capitalist traditions," then the escape from this national accounting and control will inevitably become so increasingly difficult, such a rare exception, and will probably be accompanied by such swift and severe punishment (for the armed

---

* When most of the functions of the state are reduced to this accounting and control by the workers themselves, then it ceases to be a "political state," and the "public functions will lose their political character and be transformed into simple administrative functions" (*cf.* above, Chap. IV, § 2 on Engels' polemic against the Anarchists).

workers are men of practical life, not sentimental intellectuals, and they will scarcely allow any one to trifle with them), that very soon the *necessity* of observing the simple, fundamental rules of every-day social life in common will have become a *habit*.

The door will then be wide open for the transition from the first phase of Communist society to its higher phase, and along with it to the complete withering away of the state.

CHAPTER VI

VULGARISATION OF MARX BY THE OPPORTUNISTS

THE question of the relation of the state to the social revolution, and of the social revolution to the state, like the question of revolution generally, occupied the best known theoreticians and publicists of the Second International (1889-1914) very little. But the most characteristic thing in that process of the gradual growth of opportunism, which led to the collapse of the Second International in 1914, is the circumstance that even when those people actually came into contact with this question they *tried to evade it* or else failed to notice it.

It may, in general, be said that the *evasiveness* on the question of the relation of the proletarian revolution to the state, an evasiveness which was convenient for opportunism and nourished it—resulted in a *distortion* of Marxism and in its complete vulgarisation.

To characterise, if only in brief, this lamentable process, let us take the best known theoreticians of Marxism: Plekhanov and Kautsky.

1. PLEKHANOV'S POLEMIC AGAINST THE ANARCHISTS

Plekhanov devoted a special pamphlet to the question of the relation of Anarchism to Socialism, entitled *Anarchism and Socialism*, published in German in 1894.

Plekhanov managed somehow to treat this topic without touching on the most vital, timely, and politically essential point in the struggle with Anarchism: the relation of the revolution to the state, and the question of the state in general! His pamphlet is divided into two parts: one, historical and literary, containing valuable material for the history of the ideas of Stirner, Proudhon and others; the second is philistine, and contains a clumsy dissertation on the theme that an Anarchist cannot be distinguished from a bandit.

An amusing combination of subjects and most characteristic of Plekhanov's whole activity on the eve of the revolution and during the revolutionary period in Russia. Indeed, in the years 1905 to 1917, Plekhanov showed himself to be half doctrinaire and half philistine, following politically in the wake of the bourgeoisie.

We have seen how Marx and Engels, in their polemics against the Anarchists, explained most thoroughly their views on the relation of the revolution to the state. Engels, upon the publication of Marx's *Critique of the Gotha Programme* in 1891, wrote that "we"—that is, Engels and Marx—"were then, hardly two years after the Hague Congress of the [First] International,[9] in the fiercest phase of our struggle with Bakunin and his Anarchists."

The Anarchists had tried to claim the Paris Commune as their "own," as a confirmation of their teachings, thus showing that they had not in the least understood the lessons of the Commune or the analysis of those lessons by Marx. Anarchism has failed to give anything even approaching a true solution of the concrete political problems: must the old state machinery be *shattered,* and *what* shall be put in its place?

But to speak of "Anarchism and Socialism," leaving the whole question of the state out of account and *taking no notice* of the whole development of Marxism before and after the Commune —meant an inevitable fall into opportunism. For that is just what opportunism wants—that the two questions just mentioned should *not* be raised at all. This is already a victory for opportunism.

2. KAUTSKY'S POLEMIC AGAINST THE OPPORTUNISTS

Undoubtedly an immeasurably larger number of Kautsky's works have been translated into Russian than into any other language. It is not without justification that German Social-Democrats sometimes say jokingly that Kautsky is more read in Russia than in Germany (we may say, in parentheses, that there is deeper historical significance in this joke than those who first made it suspected; for the Russian workers, having manifested in 1905 an extraordinarily strong, an unprecedented demand for the best works of the best Social-Democratic literature in the world, and having been supplied with translations and editions of these works in quantities unheard of in other countries, thereby transplanted, so to speak, with an accelerated tempo, the immense experience of a neighbouring, more advanced country to the almost virgin soil of our proletarian movement).

Besides his popularisation of Marxism, Kautsky is particularly well known in our country by his polemics against the opportunists, chiefly Bernstein. But one fact is almost unknown, which cannot be overlooked if we are to apply ourselves to the task of investigating how it was that Kautsky plunged into the unbelievably disgraceful morass of confusion and defence of social-chauvinism at a time of greatest crisis, in 1914-1915. This fact is that shortly before he came out against the best known representatives of opportunism in France (Millerand and Jaurès) and in Germany (Bernstein), Kautsky had shown very great vacillation. The Marxist journal, *Zarya*, which was published in Stuttgart in 1901-1902, and advocated revolutionary proletarian views, was forced to *polemise* against Kautsky, to characterise as "rubber-like" his evasive, temporising, and conciliatory attitude towards the opportunists as expressed in his resolution at the International Socialist Congress in Paris in 1900.[10] Letters have been published from Kautsky's pen in Germany, revealing no less hesitancy before he took the field against Bernstein.

Of immeasurably greater significance, however, is the circumstance that, in his very polemic against the opportunists, in his formulation of the question and his method of treating it, we can observe, now that we are investigating the *history* of his latest betrayal of Marxism, his systematic gravitation towards opportunism, precisely on the question of the state.

Let us take Kautsky's first big work against opportunism: *Bernstein und das sozialdemokratische Programm.* Kautsky refutes Bernstein in detail, but the characteristic thing about it is the following:

Bernstein, in his Herostrates-like famous *Voraussetzungen des Sozialismus,* accuses Marxism of *"Blanquism"* (an accusation since repeated thousands of times by the opportunists and liberal bourgeois in Russia against the representatives of revolutionary Marxism, the Bolsheviks). In this connection Bernstein dwells particularly on Marx's *The Civil War in France,* and tries—as we saw, quite unsuccessfully—to identify Marx's view of the lessons of the Commune with that of Proudhon. Bernstein pays particular attention to Marx's conclusion, emphasised by him in his 1872 preface to the *Communist Manifesto,* to the effect that "the working class cannot simply lay hold of the ready-made state machinery, and wield it for its own purposes."

The dictum "pleased" Bernstein so much that he repeated it no less than three times in his book—interpreting it in the most distorted opportunist sense.

We have seen what Marx means—that the working class must *shatter, break up, blow up* (*Sprengung*, explosion, is the expression used by Engels) the whole state machinery. But according to Bernstein it would appear as though Marx by these words warned the working class *against* excessive revolutionary zeal when seizing power.

A crasser and uglier perversion of Marx's ideas cannot be imagined.

How, then, did Kautsky act in his detailed refutation of Bernsteinism?

He avoided analysing the whole enormity of the perversion of Marxism by opportunism on this point. He cited the above-quoted passage from Engels' preface to Marx's *Civil War*, saying that, according to Marx, the working class cannot *simply* take possession of the *ready-made* state machinery, but, generally speaking, it *can* take possession of it—and that was all. As for the fact that Bernstein attributed to Marx the *direct opposite* of Marx's real views, that the real task of the proletarian revolution, as formulated by Marx ever since 1852, was to "break up" the state machinery—not a word of all this is to be found in Kautsky.

The result was that the most essential difference between Marxism and opportunism on the question of the proletarian revolution was glossed over!

"The solution of the problem of the proletarian dictatorship," wrote Kautsky *"in opposition"* to Bernstein, "we can safely leave to the future" (p. 172, German edition).

This is not a polemic *against* Bernstein, but really a *concession* to him, a surrender to opportunism; for at present the opportunists ask nothing better than to "safely leave to the future" all the fundamental questions on the tasks of the proletarian revolution.

Marx and Engels, from 1852 to 1891—for forty years—taught the proletariat that it must break up the state machinery. Kautsky, in 1899, confronted on this point with the complete betrayal of Marxism by the opportunists, fraudulently *substitutes* for the question as to whether it is necessary to break up the machinery, the question as to the concrete forms of breaking it up, and then saves himself behind the screen of the "indisputable" (and barren) philistine truth, that concrete forms cannot be known in advance!!

Between Marx and Kautsky, between their respective attitudes to the task of a proletarian party in preparing the working class for revolution, there is an abyss.

Let us take the next, more mature, work by Kautsky, also devoted, to a large extent, to a refutation of opportunist errors. This is his pamphlet, *The Social Revolution*.[11] The author chose here as his special theme the question of "the proletarian revolution" and the "proletarian régime." He gave here a great deal of valuable material; but *evaded* this question of the state. Throughout the pamphlet the author speaks of the conquest of the state power— and nothing else; that is, a formulation is chosen which makes a concession to the opportunists, since it *admits* the possibility of the conquest of power *without* the destruction of the state machinery. The very thing which Marx, in 1872, declared to be "obsolete" in the programme of the *Communist Manifesto, is revived* by Kautsky in 1902!

In the pamphlet a special section is devoted to "the forms and weapons of the social revolution." Here he speaks of the political mass strike, of civil war, and of such "instruments of force at the disposal of the modern large state as the bureaucracy and the army"; but of that which the Commune had already taught the workers, not a syllable. Evidently Engels had issued no idle warning, for the German Social-Democrats particularly, against "superstitious reverence" for the state.

Kautsky propounds the matter in the following way: the victorious proletariat, he says, "will realise the democratic programme," and he formulates its clauses. But of that which the year 1871 taught us about bourgeois democracy being replaced by a proletarian one —not a syllable. Kautsky disposes of the question by such "profound" looking banalities as:

It is obvious that we shall not attain power under the present order of things. Revolution itself presupposes a prolonged and far-reaching struggle which, as it proceeds, will change our present political and social structure.

This is undoubtedly "obvious"; as much as that horses eat oats, or that the Volga flows into the Caspian Sea. It is only a pity that he should use this empty and bombastic phrase of "far-reaching" struggle to *slur over* the question essential for the revolutionary proletariat, namely, *wherein* exactly lies this "far-reaching" nature of *its* revolution with respect to the state, with respect to democracy, as distinguished from the non-proletarian revolutions of the past.

By evading this question, Kautsky *in reality* makes a concession to opportunism in this most essential point, while declaring a terrible war against it *in words,* emphasising the importance of the "idea of revolution" (how much is this "idea" worth, if one is afraid to spread among the workers the concrete lessons of the revolution?) or declaring that "revolutionary idealism is above all," that the English workers represent now "little more than petty-bourgeois."

In a Socialist society—Kautsky writes—there can exist, side by side, the most varied forms of economic enterprises—bureaucratic [??], trade union, co-operative, private. . . . There are, for instance, such enterprises as cannot do without a bureaucratic [??] organisation: such are the railways. Here democratic organisation might take the following form: the workers elect delegates, who form something in the nature of a parliament, and this parliament determines the conditions of work, and superintends the management of the bureaucratic apparatus. Other enterprises may be transferred to the labour unions, and still others may be organised on a co-operative basis.

This reasoning is erroneous, and represents a step backward in comparison with what Marx and Engels explained in the 'seventies, using the lessons of the Commune as an example.

So far as this assumed necessity of "bureaucratic" organisation is concerned, there is no difference whatever between railways and any other enterprise of large-scale machine industry, any factory, any large store, or large-scale capitalist agricultural enterprise. The technique of all such enterprises requires the very strictest discipline, the greatest accuracy in the carrying out by every one of the work allotted to him, under peril of stoppage of the whole business or damage to mechanism or product. In all such enterprises the workers will, of course, "elect delegates who form *something in the nature of a parliament.*"

But here is the crux of the matter: this "something in the nature of a parliament" will *not* be a parliament in the sense of bourgeois-parliamentary institutions. The crux of the matter is that this "something in the nature of a parliament" will *not* merely "determine the conditions of work, and superintend the management of the bureaucratic apparatus," as imagined by Kautsky, whose ideas do not go beyond the framework of bourgeois parliamentarism. In a Socialist society, this "something in the nature of a parliament," consisting of workers' deputies, will of course determine the conditions of work, and superintend the management of the "apparatus" —*but* this apparatus will *not* be "bureaucratic." The workers, having conquered political power, will break up the old bureaucratic apparatus, they will shatter it to its very foundations, until not one stone is left upon another; and they will replace it with a new one consisting of these same workers and employees, *against* whose transformation into bureaucrats measures will at once be undertaken, as pointed out in detail by Marx and Engels: (1) not only electiveness, but also instant recall; (2) payment no higher than that of ordinary workers; (3) immediate transition to a state of things when *all* fulfil the functions of control and superintendence, so that *all* become "bureaucrats" for a time, and *no one*, therefore, can become a "bureaucrat."

Kautsky has not reflected at all on Marx's words: "The Commune was to be a working, not a parliamentary body, executive and legislative at the same time."

Kautsky has not in the least understood the difference between bourgeois parliamentarism, combining democracy (*not for the people*) with bureaucracy (*against the people*), and proletarian democracy, which will take immediate steps to cut down bureaucracy at the roots, and which will be able to carry out these measures to their conclusion, the complete destruction of bureaucracy, and the final establishment of democracy for the people.

Kautsky reveals here again the same "superstitious reverence" for the state, and "superstitious faith" in bureaucracy.

Let us pass to the last and best of Kautsky's works against the opportunists, his pamphlet, *Der Weg zur Macht* [*The Road to Power*] (which I believe has not been translated into Russian, for it came out during the severest period of reaction here, in 1909).[12] This pamphlet is a considerable step forward, inasmuch as it does not treat the revolutionary programme in general, as in the pamphlet of 1899 against Bernstein, nor the tasks of a social revolution irrespective of the time of its occurrence, as in the pamphlet, *The Social Revolution*, 1902, but the concrete conditions which compel us to recognise that the "revolutionary era" *is approaching*.

The author definitely calls attention to the intensification of class antagonisms in general and to imperialism, which plays a particularly important part in this connection. After the "revolutionary period of 1789-1871" in Western Europe, he says, an analogous period begins for the East in 1905. A world war is approaching with menacing rapidity. "The proletariat can no longer talk of premature revolution." "The revolutionary era is beginning."

These declarations are perfectly clear. The pamphlet ought to serve as a measure of comparison between the *high promise* of German Social-Democracy before the imperialist war and the depth of degradation to which it fell—Kautsky included—when the war broke out. "The present situation," Kautsky wrote in the pamphlet under consideration, "contains this danger, that we" (*i.e.*, German Social-Democracy), "may easily be considered more moderate than we are in reality." In reality, the German Social-Democratic Party turned out even more moderate and opportunist than it had seemed!

The more characteristic it is that, side by side with such definite declarations regarding the revolutionary era that had already begun, Kautsky, in the pamphlet which, he says himself, is devoted precisely to an analysis of the "political revolution," again completely dodges the question of the state.

From all these evasions of the question, omissions and equivocations, there inevitably followed that complete surrender to opportunism of which we shall soon have to speak.

German Social-Democracy, in the person of Kautsky, seems to have declared: I uphold revolutionary views (1899); I recognise, in particular, the inevitability of the social revolution of the proletariat (1902); I recognise the approach of a new revolutionary era (1909); still I disavow that which Marx said as early as 1852 —if once the question is definitely raised as to the tasks confronting a proletarian revolution in relation to the state (1912).

It was precisely in this direct form that the question was put in the polemic of Kautsky against Pannekoek.

3. KAUTSKY'S POLEMIC AGAINST PANNEKOEK

Pannekoek came out against Kautsky as one of the representatives of the "left radical" movement which counted in its ranks Rosa Luxemburg, Karl Radek, and others, and which, while upholding revolutionary tactics, was united in the conviction that Kautsky was taking a "centre" position, that he was wavering in an unprincipled manner between Marxism and opportunism. The correctness of this view was fully proved by the war, when this "centre" current or Kautskyism, wrongly called Marxist, revealed itself in all its hideous squalor.

In an article touching on the question of the state, entitled "Mass Action and Revolution" (*Neue Zeit*, 1912, XXX-2), Pannekoek characterised Kautsky's position as an attitude of "passive radicalism," as "a theory of inactive waiting." "Kautsky does not want to see the process of revolution," says Pannekoek (p. 616). In thus stating the problem, Pannekoek approached the subject which interests us, namely, the tasks of a proletarian revolution in relation to the state.

The struggle of the proletariat—he wrote—is not merely a struggle against the bourgeoisie for the purpose of acquiring state power, but a struggle *against* the state power. The content of a proletarian revolution is the destruction of the instruments of the state power, and their forcing out [literally: dissolution, *Auflösung*] by the instruments of the power of the proletariat. . . . The struggle will not end until, as its final result, the entire state organisation is destroyed. The organisation of the majority demonstrates its superiority by destroying the organisation of the ruling minority (p. 548).

The formulation in which Pannekoek presented his ideas has very great defects, but its meaning is sufficiently clear; and it is interesting to note how Kautsky combated it.

Up till now—he wrote—the difference between Social-Democrats and Anarchists has consisted in this: the former wished to conquer the state power while the latter wished to destroy it. Pannekoek wants to do both (p. 724).

If Pannekoek's exposition lacks precision and concreteness—not to speak of other defects which have no bearing on the present subject—Kautsky seized on just that one point in Pannekoek's article which is the essential principle of the whole matter; and *on this fundamental question of principle* Kautsky forsakes the Marxian position entirely and surrenders without reserve to the opportunists. His definition of the difference between Social-Democrats and Anarchists is absolutely wrong; and Marxism is thoroughly vulgarised and distorted.

The difference between the Marxists and Anarchists consists in this: (1) the former, while aiming at the complete destruction of the state, recognise that this aim can only be realised after the abolition of classes by a Socialist revolution, as the result of the establishment of Socialism, leading to the withering away of the state; the latter want the complete destruction of the state within twenty-four hours, not understanding the conditions under which such destruction can be carried out; (2) the former recognise that when once the proletariat has won political power it must utterly break up the old state machinery, and substitute for it a new one consisting of an organisation of armed workers, after the type of the

Commune; the latter, while advocating the destruction of the state machinery, have absolutely no clear idea as to *what* the proletariat will put in its place and *how* it will use its revolutionary power; the Anarchists even reject the utilisation by the revolutionary proletariat of state power, the revolutionary dictatorship of the proletariat; (3) the former insist upon making use of the modern state as a means of preparing the workers for revolution; the latter reject this.

In this controversy it is Pannekoek, not Kautsky, who represents Marxism, for it was Marx who taught that it is not enough for the proletariat simply to conquer state power in the sense of the old state apparatus passing into new hands, but that the proletariat must break up, smash this apparatus and replace it by a new one.

Kautsky goes over from Marxism to the opportunists, because, in his hands, this destruction of the state machinery, which is utterly inacceptable to the opportunists, completely disappears, and there remains for them a loophole in that they can interpret "conquest" as the simple gaining of a majority.

To cover up his distortion of Marxism, Kautsky acts like the religious debater in the village: he advances "quotations" from Marx himself. Marx wrote in 1850 of the necessity of "a decisive centralisation of power in the hands of the state"; and Kautsky triumphantly asks: does Pannekoek want to destroy "centralism"?

This is nothing but sleight-of-hand, similar to Bernstein's identification of the views of Marxism and Proudhonism on federalism versus centralism.

Kautsky's "quotation" is neither here nor there. The new state machinery admits centralism as much as the old; if the workers voluntarily unify their armed forces, this will be centralism, but it will be based on the "complete destruction" of the centralised state apparatus—the army, police, bureaucracy. Kautsky acts just like a swindler when he ignores the perfectly well known arguments of Marx and Engels on the Commune and comes out with a quotation which has nothing to do with the case.

He continues:

Perhaps Pann..koek wants to abolish the state functions of the officials? But we cannot do v/ithout officials even in our party and trade union organisations, much less in the state administration. Our programme demands, not abolition of state officials, but their election by the people. . . . It is not a question as to the precise form which the administrative apparatus will take in the "future state," but as to whether our political struggle destroys [literally: dissolves, *"auflöst"*] the state *before we have conquered it* [Kautsky's italics]. What ministry with its officials could be abolished? [There follows an enumeration of the ministries of education, justice, finance and war.] No, not one of the present ministries will be removed by our political struggles against the government. . . . I repeat, to avoid misunderstanding: it is not here a question of what form a victorious Social-Democracy will give to the "future state," but of how our opposition changes the present state (p. 725).

This is an obvious trick: *revolution* was the question Pannekoek raised. Both the title of his article and the passages quoted above show that clearly. When Kautsky jumps over to the question of "opposition," he changes the revolutionary point of view for the opportunist. What he says is: opposition *now,* and a special talk about the matter *after* we have won power. *The revolution has vanished!* That is precisely what the opportunists wanted.

Opposition and general political struggle are beside the point; we are concerned with the *revolution.* And revolution consists in the proletariat's *destroying* the "administrative apparatus" and the *whole* state machinery, and replacing it by a new one consisting of the armed workers. Kautsky reveals a "superstitious reverence" for ministries; but why can they not be replaced, say, by commissions of specialists working under sovereign all-powerful Soviets of Workers' and Soldiers' Deputies?

The essence of the matter is not at all whether the "ministries" will remain or "commissions of specialists" or any other kind of institutions will exist; this is quite unimportant. The main thing is whether the old state machinery (connected by thousands of threads with the bourgeoisie and saturated through and through with routine and inertia) shall remain or be *destroyed* and replaced by a *new* one. A revolution must not consist in a new class ruling, governing with the help of the *old* state machinery, but in this class *smashing* this machinery and ruling, governing by means of *new* machinery. This *fundamental* idea of Marxism Kautsky either slurs over or has not understood at all.

His question about officials shows clearly that he does not understand the lessons of the Commune or the teachings of Marx. "We cannot do without officials even in our party and trade union organisations. . . ."

We cannot do without officials *under capitalism, under the rule of the bourgeoisie.* The proletariat is oppressed, the labouring masses are enslaved by capitalism. Under capitalism, democracy is narrowed, crushed, curtailed, mutilated by all the conditions of wage-slavery, the poverty and misery of the masses. This is the reason, and the only reason, why the officials of our political parties and trade unions become corrupt—or, more precisely, tend to become corrupt—under capitalist conditions, why they show a tendency to turn into bureaucrats, *i.e.*, privileged persons detached from the masses, and standing *above* the masses.

That is the *essence* of bureaucracy, and until the capitalists have been expropriated and the bourgeoisie overthrown, *even* proletarian officials will inevitably be to some extent "bureaucratised."

From what Kautsky says, one might think that if elective officials remain under Socialism, bureaucrats and bureaucracy will also remain! That is entirely incorrect. Marx took the example of the Commune to show that under Socialism the functionaries cease to be "bureaucrats" and "officials"—they change *in the degree* as election is supplemented by the right of instant recall; when, *besides this,* their pay is brought down to the level of the pay of the average worker; when, *besides this,* parliamentary institutions are replaced by "working bodies, executive and legislative at the same time."

All Kautsky's arguments against Pannekoek, and particularly his splendid point that we cannot do without officials even in our parties and trade unions, show, in essence, that Kautsky is repeating the old "arguments" of Bernstein against Marxism in general. Bernstein's renegade book, *Evolutionary Socialism,* is an attack on "primitive" democracy—"doctrinaire democracy" as he calls it— imperative mandates, functionaries without pay, impotent central representative bodies, and so on. To prove that "primitive democracy" is worthless, Bernstein refers to the British trade union experience, as interpreted by the Webbs. Seventy-odd years of development "in absolute freedom" (p. 137, German edition), have, he avers, convinced the trade unions that primitive democracy is useless, and led them to replace it with ordinary parliamentarism combined with bureaucracy.

In reality the trade unions developed not "in absolute freedom" *but in complete capitalist enslavement,* under which one, naturally, "cannot do without" concessions to the prevailing evil, force, falsehood, exclusion of the poor from the affairs of the "higher" administration. Under Socialism much of the "primitive" democracy is inevitably revived, since, for the first time in the history of civilised society, the *mass* of the population rises to *independent* participation, not only in voting and elections, *but also in the every-day administration of affairs*. Under Socialism, *all* will take a turn in management, and will soon become accustomed to the idea of no managers at all.

Marx's critico-analytical genius perceived in the practical measures of the Commune that revolutionary *turning point* of which the opportunists are afraid, and which they do not want to recognise, out of cowardice, out of reluctance to break irrevocably with the bourgeoisie, and which the Anarchists do not want to perceive, either through haste or a general lack of understanding of the conditions of great social mass transformations. "One must not even think of such a thing as destroying the old state machinery, for how shall we do without ministries and without officials?" argues the opportunist, saturated through and through with philistinism, and in reality not merely devoid of faith in revolution, in the creative power of revolution, but actually in mortal dread of it (like our Mensheviks and Socialist-Revolutionaries).

"One must think *only* of the destruction of the old state machinery; never mind searching for *concrete* lessons in earlier proletarian revolutions and analysing *with what* and *how* to replace what has been destroyed," argues the Anarchist (the best of the Anarchists, of course, and not those who, with Messrs. Kropotkins and Co., follow in the train of the bourgeoisie); consequently, the tactics of the Anarchist become the tactics of *despair* instead of a revolutionary grappling with concrete problems—ruthlessly courageous and at the same time cognisant of the practical conditions under which the masses progress.

Marx teaches us to avoid both kinds of error; he teaches us unswerving courage in destroying the entire old state machinery, and at the same time shows us how to put the situation concretely: the Commune was able, within a few weeks, to *start* building a *new*, proletarian state machinery by introducing such and such measures to secure a wider democracy, and to uproot bureaucracy. Let us learn revolutionary courage from the Communards; let us see in their practical measures *an outline* of practically urgent and immediately possible measures, and then, following this road, we shall arrive at the complete destruction of bureaucracy.

The possibility of such destruction is assured by the fact that Socialism will shorten the working day, raise the *masses* to a new life, create such conditions for the *majority* of the population as to enable *everybody,* without exception, to perform "state functions," and this will lead to a *complete withering away* of every state in general.

> The object of a general strike—Kautsky continues—can never be to destroy the state, but only to wring concessions from the government on some particular question, or to replace a hostile government with one willing to meet the proletariat half way [*entgegenkommend*]. . . . But never, under any conditions, can it (a proletarian victory over a hostile government) lead to the *destruction* of the state power; it can lead only to a certain *shifting* [*Verschiebung*] of forces *within the state* power. . . . The aim of our political struggle, then, remains as before, the conquest of state power by means of gaining a majority in parliament, and the conversion of parliament into the master of the government (pp. 726, 727, 732).

This is nothing but the most clear and vulgar opportunism: a repudiation of revolution in deeds, while accepting it in words. Kautsky's imagination goes no further than a "government . . . willing to meet the proletariat half way"; this is a step backward to philistinism compared with 1847, when the *Communist Manifesto* proclaimed "the organisation of the proletariat as the ruling class."

Kautsky will have to realise his beloved "unity" with the Scheidemanns, Plekhanovs and Vanderveldes, all of whom will agree to fight for a government "meeting the proletariat half way."

But we shall go forward to a break with these traitors to Socialism, and we shall fight for complete destruction of the old state machinery, in such a way that the armed proletariat itself *is the government.* Which is a very different thing.

Kautsky may enjoy the pleasant company of the Legiens, Davids, Plekhanovs, Potresovs, Tseretelis and Chernovs, who are quite willing to work for the "shifting of the relation of forces within the state," for "gaining a majority in parliament, and the conversion of parliament into the master of the government." A most worthy object, wholly acceptable to the opportunists, in which everything remains within the framework of a bourgeois parliamentary republic.

We shall go forward to a break with the opportunists; and the whole of the class-conscious proletariat will be with us—not for a "shifting of the relation of forces," but for the *overthrow of the bourgeoisie,* the *destruction* of bourgeois parliamentarism, for a democratic republic after the type of the Commune, or a republic of Soviets of Workers' and Soldiers' Deputies, the revolutionary dictatorship of the proletariat.

To the right of Kautsky there are, in international Socialism, such tendencies as the *Sozialistische Monatshefte* [Socialist Monthly] in Germany (Legien, David, Kolb, and many others, including the Scandinavians, Stauning and Branting); the followers of Jaurès and Vandervelde in France and Belgium; Turati, Treves, and other representatives of the Right Wing of the Italian party; the Fabians and "Independents" (the Independent Labour Party, always dependent, as a matter of fact, on the Liberals) in England; and the like. All these gentry, while playing a great, very often a predominant rôle, in parliamentary work and in the journalism of the party, reject outright the dictatorship of the proletariat and carry out a policy of unconcealed opportunism. In the eyes of these gentry, the "dictatorship" of the proletariat "contradicts" democracy!! There is really no essential difference between them and the petty-bourgeois democrats.

Taking these circumstances into consideration, we have a right to conclude that the Second International, in the persons of the overwhelming majority of its official representatives, has completely sunk into opportunism. The experience of the Commune has been not only forgotten, but distorted. Far from inculcating into the workers' minds the idea that the time is near when they are to rise up and smash the old *state* machinery and substitute for it a new one, thereby making their political domination the foundation for a Socialist reconstruction of society, they have actually taught the workers the direct opposite of this, and represented the "conquest of power" in a way that left thousands of loopholes for opportunism.

The distortion and hushing up of the question as to the relation of a proletarian revolution to the state could not fail to play an immense rôle at a time when the states, with their swollen military apparatus as a consequence of imperialist rivalry, had become monstrous military beasts devouring the lives of millions of people, in order to decide whether England or Germany—this or that finance capital—should dominate the world.*

* The manuscript continues:

CHAPTER VII
EXPERIENCE OF THE RUSSIAN REVOLUTIONS OF 1905 AND 1917

THE subject indicated in the title of this chapter is so vast that volumes can and must be written about it. In the present pamphlet it will be necessary to confine ourselves, naturally, to the most important lessons of the experience, those touching directly upon the tasks of the proletariat in a revolution relative to state power. . . . [Here the manuscript breaks off.—*Ed.*]

POSTSCRIPT TO THE FIRST EDITION

THIS pamphlet was written in August and September, 1917. I had already drawn up the plan for the next, the seventh chapter, on the "Experience of the Russian Revolutions of 1905 and 1917." But, outside of the title, I did not succeed in writing a single line of the chapter; what "interfered" was the political crisis—the eve of the October Revolution of 1917. Such "interference" can only be welcomed. However, the second part of the pamphlet (devoted to the "Experience of the Russian Revolutions of 1905 and 1917,") will probably have to be put off for a long time. It is more pleasant and useful to go through the "experience of the revolution" than to write about it.

THE AUTHOR.

PETROGRAD, December 13, 1917.

Written in August-September, 1917.
First published as a pamphlet by the publishing firm *Zhizn i Znaniye*, 1918.

EXPLANATORY NOTES *

1. *State and Revolution* was written by Lenin during August-September, 1917, while he was living in hiding in Helsingfors. It was not published, however, until 1918. According to the draft of the original plan made by Lenin, the work was to contain not only a theoretical analysis of the theory of the state by Marx and Engels, but also a consideration of "the experience of the Russian Revolutions of 1905 and 1917" from the point of view of this theory. But the October Revolution and the necessity to devote every effort to the immediate practical work interfered with the conclusion of the work begun.—p. 5.

2. The Thirty Years' War (1618-1648), which was caused by the struggle of the European powers for hegemony within the feudally-dismembered Germany and on the coast of the Baltic Sea, resulted in complete ruin and disaster for Germany.—p. 19.

3. *The Gotha Programme* was adopted in 1875 at the unity congress in Gotha at which the two factions of German Socialists, the Lassalleans and the Eisenachers, merged into the Social-Democratic Workers' Party of Germany. The programme officially remained in force until the convention of the party in Erfurt in 1891, when it was replaced with a new programme (the Erfurt Programme). Marx and Engels subjected the Gotha Programme to most severe criticism.—p. 20.

4. "They should not have taken up arms"—the words of G. Plekhanov about the December, 1905, armed uprising.—p. 32.

5. The Erfurt Programme, which in the epoch of the II International was considered the most consistent programme from the point of view of Marxism and which for a long time served as a model for all other Social-Democratic parties, including the R. S.-D. L. P., was adopted at the congress of the German Social-Democracy in Erfurt, October 14-20, 1891, in place of the obsolete Gotha Programme (1875), which was the result of a compromise of two trends in German Socialism (Lassalleans and Eisenachers).—p. 57.

6. See Engels' Introduction to the 1891 edition of the *Civil War in France*. —p. 62.

7. Lenin here and further on makes a slip of the pen: the "historic" speech of Tsereteli was made not on June 22, but on June 24. For further details about this speech, see V. I. Lenin, *Revolution of 1917, Collected Works*, Volume XX, note 255.—p. 63.

* Fuller notes on *State and Revolution* will be found in the Explanatory Notes of *Toward the Seizure of Power*, Lenin's *Collected Works*, Vol. XXI, Book II.

8. It must be kept in mind that the figures quoted by Lenin as possible rates of wages are given in the paper currency of the second half of 1917. *State and Revolution* was written in August, 1917, when the value of the Russian paper ruble had fallen to less than a third of its face value.—p. 64.

9. The Hague (V) Congress of the First International (1872), attended by Marx and Engels, was almost entirely devoted to the struggle with the Bakuninists. On the motion of Vaillant, the Congress adopted a resolution recognising the necessity of political struggle, contrary to the opinion of the Bakuninists. Bakunin and several of his adherents were expelled from the International. The Hague Congress was the last congress of the First International in Europe.—p. 87.

10. Concerning the Fifth International Socialist Congress held in Paris (1901), and the Kautsky resolution on Millerandism adopted by it, see V. I. Lenin, *The Iskra Period, Collected Works*, Volume IV, note 35.—p. 88.

11. Lenin refers to Karl Kautsky's book *Die Soziale Revolution, I. Sozialreform und Soziale Revolution, II. Am Tage nach der Sozialen Revolution* (Social Revolution, I. Social Reform and Social Revolution, II. On the Morrow of the Social Revolution). Throughout the entire *State and Revolution*, Lenin almost everywhere quotes foreign authors from the original, making his own translations from German for each quotation, apparently not being satisfied with the existing translations.—p. 90.

12. Lenin refers to Kautsky's book; *Der Weg zur Macht. Politische Betrachtungen in die Revolution* (*The Road to Power. Political Considerations in the Revolution*), Berlin, 1909.—p. 92.